WHO KILLED MY WIFE?

The Unsolved Murder of Bernita White

BY

ARTIS

WHITE

WHO KILLED BERNITA?

DISCLAIMER

This book is designed to provide information about the subject matter covered. It is sold with the understanding that the publisher and author are not engaged in rendering legal, or other professional services. If legal or other expert assistance is required, the services of a competent professional should be sought.

Every effort has been made to make this book as complete and as accurate as possible. However, there may be mistakes both typographical and in content. Therefore, this text should be used only as a general resource and not as the ultimate source of any legal investigation.

The purpose of this book is to educate and enlighten. The author and Artistic Expressions LLC shall have neither liability nor responsibility to any person or entity with respect to any loss or damage caused or alleged to be caused directly or indirectly by the information contained in this book. If you do not wish to be bound by the above, you may return this book to the publisher for a full refund.

Some of the names in this book have been changed to maintain the privacy and confidentiality of those individuals.

Although the author and publisher have made every effort to ensure the accuracy and completeness of information contained in this book, we assume no responsibility for errors, inaccuracies, omissions, or any inconsistency herein. Any slights of people, places, or organizations are unintentional.

Published by Artistic Expressions LLC
5115 Deanna Drive, Lansing, MI 48917
www.artisticexpressions.org

ISBN 09722480-0-5
LCCN 20002093137

FOREWORD

The purpose of this book is to allow Artis White to be able to tell the truth. The truth about what really happened during those unforetold tragic seconds on June 23, 2001, when his wife, Bernita White was murdered. The truth about what happened during the hours, days, weeks and months to follow.

It is for something good and beneficial to come out of the senseless death of a beautiful and loving woman. And, it is for other victims, families, and friends who are caught in the unsuspecting wiles of an imperfect world of justice.

I have known the author personally for twenty years. Like Artis, I, too, am part of the criminal justice system. To those of us who are part of it on a day-to-day basis, its imperfections are as obvious as the imperfections of the individuals who comprise the justice system. You, the unsuspecting citizen, have no idea of what you will encounter if you end up in the spider web referred to as the wheels of justice. This book describes the pitfalls of the criminal justice system that are bestowed upon unlikely victims. Artis was at the time of his wife's murder and still is, a Michigan State Trooper.

Who better would understand the justice system and how the game is played. Yet he, too, like other innocent victims was caught in the web of justice and felt firsthand the results of an imperfect system made up of imperfect people.

Artis wrote this book so the truth would be revealed in its entirety. Understand, after reading this book you will not have the satisfaction of knowing the answers. The answers are not there. A happy ending does not exist. The justice system was incapable of providing the truth in this case. Even though the justice system did not produce the answers in this case, it is still the best we have at this time. Without it, society would be in chaos.

By reading this book, you learn the truth and gain insight into the real people involved. You will learn about Artis L. White, Jr., the husband, father, police officer, friend and suspect.

The Honorable Judge Wade McCree

PREFACE

At some point, you will encounter a police officer. Perhaps you will attend a crime prevention seminar or belong to a committee on which a police officer serves. And most often, your experience will be a pleasant one. But you may also meet a police officer during a traffic violation and even then, most of the time you will come away without thinking negatively about the police officer. However, the fact is most of us hope we never have to be involved with the police. If for no other reason than it looks bad. And if we have done something wrong, we hope, somehow, we'll get away with it. Sometimes we do, sometimes we don't. But if the same scenario happens to someone else, the common response is, "He must have had it coming or the police would not be involved." It is a common feeling.

Most of America has accepted police work as a difficult, thankless job. This is true. The perception of a police officer has changed since the early 1900's. For example, it was commonplace in that era, for restaurant owners to provide a police officer with a free lunch or dinner to supplement their low salaries. It was even common for business owners to give a police officer a set of keys to the establishment for foot patrol after hours. All that has changed. This day and age, a business owner is more inclined to secure his own premises without depending on police presence after hours.

The salary for law enforcement officers has increased, making a career in law enforcement appealing. There's no need for free food but that tradition continues today with discounts offered to officers who dine in restaurants adorned in full uniform as a deterrent to crime. This practice is accepted by some police departments. Other departments believe this can lure police officers away from fair enforcement of the law. The phrase "thin blue line" is a result of that kind of thinking.

We ("We" in the sense that I am a police officer and a citizen) hire the police to enforce the laws we create. Police go out and do our "dirty work." There is nothing magical that separates a police officer from right and wrong; and therefore there is no line drawn in the sand (real or imaginary) that distinguishes when an officer has gone "over the edge." Private citizens, not the police, make the laws. When the police make mistakes, we are furious and demand reform but only for a short while. Therefore, the "thin blue line" can easily be stepped over or ignored. An individual, civilian, or enlisted officer may know what is good or bad, as each person learns at an early age, what is right and wrong. However, the written word of the law allows for interpretation but does not explain the difference between right and wrong. Individuals must draw their own conclusions based on life experiences. With that understood, we can rationalize there is not much difference between the average citizen and a police officer. However, when a police officer intentionally commits a wrongful act, he should be held to a higher standard because of the amount of trust and power of discretion that comes with his profession.

Nobody likes crime; therefore, we have no other choice than to employ police officers to maintain law and order. Sometimes, the common practice is to close one eye and wink the other when an officer crosses the "line" because we understand the difficulties of the profession. This gesture of forgiveness allows an easy opportunity for an unmotivated, inexperienced officer to hide in a department that is willing to overlook his problems in order to avoid public scrutiny. It is up to citizens and individual police departments to make sure this does not happen. Police are only the messengers carrying our message; however, a police department must accept the blame when an officer is not courageous enough to admit that he enforced his own internal values and decisions and not the law. If we, as citizens, do not like the results, it is our responsibility to say so. Everyone must be held accountable for his or her actions, no matter what the profession, especially when the result of that action has a severe impact on someone else. If a police department or its members are allowed to operate in a manner unchecked, it creates a playground for poor attitudes, jealousy, vengeance and un-professionalism to run rampant. The result: uninspired officers motivated by personal career advancement, greed and a sense of invincibility.

Citizen response and police departments committed to justice can make the difference and the death of Bernita White will not go unsolved.

The truth is there...find it.

INTRODUCTION

Murder has an affect on everyone. It's the most heinous crime with the most extensive history, and the penalty for committing it is capital punishment. So, it follows that murder has more impact on society than any other crime. Eighty percent of murders are domestics: husband-wife, girlfriend-boyfriend. Most murders are spontaneous and not premeditated. A large percentage of the time, murder is the result of a mistake. The majority of homicides are committed by a perpetrator who knows the victim and, in a time of anger, does something unexpected and irrational.

Statistics do not show the unnecessary painful suffering to the families of the victims. There is no way to gauge the amount of trauma that follows a murder. People feel powerless and helpless, especially when they have no voice or when there is no immediate resolution of justice. When the police are free to commit investigative errors, there is no appeal process. It's simply too late. What could have been resolved is now a cold case and the family of the victim lives a continuous nightmare.

Solved or unsolved, murder in any form still has an affect. If you know the victim, you will experience a lifetime of pain. If you do not know the victim, your 20 seconds of curiosity will be recycled with the morning newspaper. What is the difference between the murder of a rich person and a poor person, an unknown and a celebrity? What causes a police department to spend more man-hours to find the truth and less time convincing the public they are doing the best they can?

Take a moment to review the Chandra Levy case. The case is indeed a very awful, horrible, and senseless crime. I feel for the family. Looking at the case, at least from a media perspective, there is a sense of popularity. How much time did that police department spend investigating the other, very similar murders with the same motive? How many investigative hours were spent on Alison Thresher, Dean Raley, Joyce Chiang, Christine Mirzayan, and Susan Sexton? All of these women were murdered or have been missing since 1989 from the same area where Chandra's body was found. Is it the pressure from the Levy family (And you best believe they are putting the pressure on!) to solve the case, or is it the celebrity status of Congressman Gary Condit who was indicated as a possible suspect?

We live in a world where the wheels of justice can turn so slowly that nothing happens and justice is held at bay until the wheels rust and freeze up. I believe that all the wheels rusted to a stand still in Bernita White's investigation. I am not the only one who feels this case is not getting the proper attention it needs. Whether it is the lack of celebrity status or public pressure, the interest in solving this case died one year after Bernita did. The task force working on this case simply gave up when the opportunity for glory and fame smoldered along with the lack of evidence against a police officer on the "short list of suspects." If you, the reader, are thumbing through this book looking for the answer to "Who Killed My Wife?" you will not find it here. There **is** an answer. The answer begins locally and ends globally and it is there inside the truth.

The truth is there...find it.

DEDICATION

For my daughters who experienced the greatest loss anyone could suffer.

ACKNOWLEDGEMENT

This expression of gratitude is severely inadequate to express my appreciation for those who made this book possible. For my family, I cannot say enough. I won't even try. For my true (albeit smaller in number now) friends, thank you for your comfort and staying power. For Richard Baldwin, author/teacher, you may never realize how you motivated me. Thank you Gail Garber for editing my book and thank you M. "Sam" Nesbitt for the typesetting and book cover. The two of you no doubt had a very difficult task considering my talents as an author, or lack thereof. Marcia, you are my inspiration as well as my moral compass. For Lansing Police and Michigan State Police authorities and their refusal to listen to witnesses and accept the truth—you deserve full acknowledgement for that.

AUTHOR'S NOTE

This is a true story. The facts are documented. Newspaper articles, personal interviews and public surveys have been slightly condensed in the interest of space and to avoid repetition. Several last names have been omitted to protect sources of information whose identifications are not part of public record. The dialogue represented in this book was constructed from available documents, court filings, personal recollections, or reconstructed from the memories of the participants. This book is intended to raise questions. It is my hope that people will come forward with answers to questions the police authorities refuse to ask; the proper ones. Everyday I wake up and look in the mirror to see the reflection of the reader of this book. I go for a walk in the park and I walk in the shoes of the victim. I stand still, do nothing and I can hear the call of every unsolved murder victim. Ten percent of people in this world make things happen. Forty percent of people in this world wait for something to happen. Fifty percent of the people in this world wonder what happened. That's too late.

The truth is there... find it.

http://www.artisticexpressions.org

A woman in her forties is killed with a high-powered rifle while walking with her daughter and friends at a crowded public zoo in Lansing, Michigan. Her husband, a detective with the state police, is a suspect in the murder as the couple's pending amicable divorce is the only apparent motive. No other suspects are developed in this case. Investigators' arrogance, jealousy and lack of training cause them to pursue a cold trail that leads further away from the victim's murderer.

For You

Her day started out exciting
but ended very frightening

The way her life was shattered
forever in our minds scatters

The way her life was taken
will never be forsaken

Her sudden death took our breath
but not our memories

Her death is a mystery
and making our family happiness to misery

It's hard to stay strong
knowing what the person did was wrong

Knowing he's still out there
but no one knows where

Bernita was such a pretty black women inside and out
that didn't have too many doubts

She was very intelligent,
talented with elegance

She was a good soul
her love never grew old

She had a lot of pride,
but never keeping it inside

Whatever she took part in
she put her heart in

You would never know why
she acted so shy

She would be quiescent,
not saying much, always silent

She was the type of person
to bring a smile from a frown

She never forgot the main priority
in her life, her children and being a wife

She was revered, loved and cherished
and now she's in a distance

That's why she is loved so much
because of the hearts she touched

Saying the word good-bye,
isn't so easy without letting out a cry but...

We'll always love you, Bernita
We'll never forget you, and
We'll always keep your spirit with us

Love, The Family

CHAPTER ONE

"There is nothing we cannot live down, rise above
and overcome."   — Ella Wheeler Wilcox

There she was, on that table in front of me. Motionless.
Neglected. Like a balloon. A dreadful, dreadful, balloon.
Swollen but wrinkled. A motionless balloon, like the kind you
see the day after your kid's birthday party, rolling around on
the floor. Dejected. My heart is nothing like a balloon for it is
heavy. That heavy sensation that beats in your neck and makes
your underarms tingle and your nose run. Now I look back at
the times we shared as husband and wife, Father and Mother,
Ambros and Boop. I never knew why she called me Ambros.
I think that was her favorite name, or was she ribbing on me
for something from the past?

  *What am I going to tell my daughters? When it all
boils down to it, this room, this hospital room is my safe
haven. For when I walk out that door I have some explaining
to do to my seven and five year-old daughters.*

How do you tell your kids their mother is dead? Of course, she is dead. She has to be. I was told it was a shot from a high-powered rifle. Of course, she is dead. Nobody gets wounded from those things. What do I tell the kids?

I don't know how to handle this. Heck, when our pet rabbit died, we bought a dog. When all of our plants in the garden died, we made a new garden. You can't replace a mother like you do a dog or a garden. Who's going to do their hair? I don't know anything about little girls' hair. I'm a "hands on" dad for sure. I bathe them when they are dirty, feed them when they are hungry, bandage them when they are hurt, and stay home with them when they are sick. I do all of the cooking, cleaning and washing clothes if only to set a good example for my daughters. The fact remains. I can't do hair. I'm handicapped, a nothing, no good father and it's going to show when they walk out of the house looking like a combination of Bozo the Clown and Pippi Longstockings.

"Mr. White, Mr. White, sir. Over here. We need you to identify the body," one of the doctors said.

You can think about dogs, gardens and how to do hair all you want. But nothing, I mean, nothing, brings you back to the present like those words. Oh sure, I've seen dead people. As a Detective Sergeant for the Michigan State Police, I have seen many things that other people have not seen.

You learn how to separate your emotions from the job, but you can't pull yourself away from this. It's no writing a report and on to the next adventure, Mr. Super

WHO KILLED MY WIFE?

Cop. No sir, Mr. Hotshot Detective. You are in the safety of this room for now, but you will soon have to face those children of yours.

"Yes. It's her. It's Bernita White. I'm her husband," I said after what seemed like a long pause.

Why are there so many people in this room? Who are all these people with bad acting skills? Who are these actors who are trying to act like they are very sorry for what happened? Police officers are the worst. With a little training, you can see right past their facade. You can see they really don't care. If it doesn't provide them with any glory or overtime, Coppers don't want anything to do with it. (Been there. It's part of the game.) At least the Victim Advocates in the room have better acting skills. I trust them. They volunteer.

*Now comes all the "Sorry about your loss." "We did everything we could." "You are going to be okay." What script **are** they reading from?*

Maybe I'm bitter about the whole thing. I ask myself why did it have to be her? Out of hundreds of people at the Potter Park Zoo, why did it have to be her? Who would want to kill her? Why couldn't I have been there to fire back? I could have at least shot in the general direction so that punk ass son of a bitch would know that somebody knows who he is. He'll get his all right.

Wait. I never use foul language. What are all these people still doing in the room? We all know what complications stand outside this room — a seven year-old and a five year-old complication.

Why did they leave that tube in her mouth for me to see? It's like that tube took all the air out of the balloon. Don't they have any common decency or do they think that Mr. Tough Guy Detective can handle it? Yes, she is dead.

The credits are rolling up at the end of her movie, but I'm just starting mine. That was not the last I saw of her.

I see that image everyday.

CHAPTER TWO

"Now comes the mystery." — Henry Ward Beecher

Life is like a 100-yard dash with birth the starting gun and death the tape. The gun went off for me 42 years ago on March 23, 1960. I was a young Black kid growing up in the middle of Detroit, Michigan. I survived, which is sometimes a difficult thing to do for inner city kids. I give that credit to my parents Mary White and Artis Sr. who moved me away from Detroit before puberty.

We lived on a 100-acre farm in Bostic, North Carolina. There we raised and sold produce right off the farm. That was quite an accomplishment for a city boy whose only view of vegetation was dandelions and vandalized maple trees. You feel rather trapped like an insect in a jar with no air holes in the city. But in the country, there is nothing but country! The hills roll on forever. No restrictions, no glass jars, just vegetation and all the air holes you need.

I despised it. I'll never do it again. Farming has to be the most difficult and unappreciated profession in the world. With the exception of ministers, rabbis, clergy, priests or the likes, no other profession has more faith than a farmer.

A farmer plants his crop with the faith that there will be enough sun, rain, and cow manure (that's what we used for fertilizer) for his crops to grow and sell in the big city so that he has enough money to feed his family. Just like his crops, the farmer will perish for lack of rain, sun and cow patties. That wasn't the life for a boy who just reached puberty but it was a lesson in life for me, to appreciate everything in life.

I gained my appreciation and respect for life on that 100-acre farm with my mother, father and younger brother Mark. The hard work, closeness of family, friends and neighbors and the uncertainty of the future are lessons I learned. These attributes I would find useful as one of Michigan State Police's finest. (I wouldn't know that until later.) I carried my family values through East Rutherford High School in Forrest City, North Carolina to Appalachian State University.

At 23, I came back to Detroit to live with my oldest sister Angela Piggee, her husband and kids, Reginald Sr., Mia, and Reginald Jr., respectfully. I attended Wayne State University, where I gained a fondness for acting. It wasn't until years later that I developed my curiosity for police work.

After a string of six years of security guard jobs, an enlistment of six years in the Michigan Army National Guard, and four years with Electronic Data Systems Corporate

Security and ownership of a private detective firm, I was accepted into the 104th Trooper Recruit School for the Michigan State Police (MSP) in 1988. I married Bernita a year later on November 25, 1989.

I met Bernita while both of us were working at J.C. Penney, part time. I was working plain-clothes security. Bernita was working ladies' handbags. I had the freedom of the whole store. Didn't matter to her. She sent one of her friends over to get me as I conveniently always made myself available. No thief ever stole from ladies' handbags with me patrolling the area. I went over to see her, looking as important and official as I could. We just stood there for a while, and then we talked. I spoke first.

"How are you?" I said, as any gentleman would.

"Fine," she said with a soft voice. She always had a soft voice.

"So, one of your soldiers escorted me over here," I said.

"That was Amy. She still goes to high school. Well, do you want my phone number?"

"Yes," I said without hesitation. That was it. That's all it took. She wrote her phone number on a J.C. Penney check routing slip. I still have that slip.

Bernita wasn't much for playing and toying around. She was very quiet and reserved. "Quiet Storm" is what she called herself. Even though we started seeing each other right away, it was a slow process to learn anything about her. When

I first started seeing her, she was living with her boyfriend, Paul. Bernita told me the reason she was living with Paul was because she had problems at home. It was never quite clear what the problems were.

Later after we were married, she would not talk about it even during therapy sessions. These problems would haunt her for years. I didn't know much about Paul other than he was a good friend of Brian's, Bernita's brother-in-law. I met him once. He only had one arm. Bernita was terrified of the prosthetic Paul would hang in the closet when he wasn't using it. That was the only thing I knew about Paul. I was curious as to why she lived with him because she told me she was never going to marry him.

"What makes you want to shack up with him?" I curiously asked.

"I didn't have anywhere else to stay."

"What's wrong with home?"

"I don't have any more money. I was just staying with him until things got better."

I noticed the past tense in her voice. From that point, we started dating each other. We were married on November 25, 1989. Bernita had very few close friends. I am not as close to her family as I would like. She never wanted to talk about her family or herself. I was always uncomfortable with that.

Her father, Bennie, Sr. worked as a used car salesman years ago. A few years ago, he was arrested and sent to Jackson

Prison for credit card fraud. The details were never told to me but he was on probation through the tether program, a program where the violator must wear an electronic tracking device around his ankle and report his presence accurately via telephone. Of course, that made for long holidays at the dinner table with yours truly. What does a police detective say to a felonious father-in-law who is on the tether program?

There were six children in Bernita's family: Bennie Jr., the oldest, Bernadette, Bernita, Belinda, Bridget and Makhia. Bernadette is an easygoing, easy talking woman who could pass as anybody's big sister. She is a married mother of two boys and her family is doing well. I always admired her strategies in raising two scrapping boys. Of all the family members, I have always felt most comfortable talking to her. She reminded me of my oldest sister at times.

I probably spent more time talking with Belinda than any other family member. Belinda followed Bernita in birth order and was the sister she was closest to. But I always felt that Bernita didn't always share things with Belinda either. Harold, Belinda's husband, and I have had several conversations about our wives and the fact that they didn't share information about their family. We always felt that they kept secrets from us. Harold is an agent for the Federal Government. That gave our two families something in common until this incident broke us apart. Bernita's death was difficult for Belinda to accept. To this day, Belinda believes I am responsible for Bernita's death.

Bernita's brother, Bennie Jr., and I may have had two conversations ever. One conversation was concerning how he was going to get rich quick by some extraordinary mysterious means and the other was how on occasion, he outsmarted the police. I didn't know whether to be entertained by his strategies or arrest him for excited utterance. I'm sure he does not stay in touch with his family. No one ever talks about him.

Bernita's sister, Bridget, was not someone I ever talked to much. She always seemed nice enough when I did. Bridget was the youngest of the family before Makhia was adopted. Makhia still lives at home with Bennie Sr.

Bernita's mother Barbara was a dear, dear lady. She was always open for conversation. Ms. Sims held the family together. She was constantly doing something. Whether it was a church function or a home project, she was always busy.

"Hey there kiddo," she would always say. She would make a comment about how well our house looked or how busy I must be. We will all miss her. Ms. Sims passed away on the day Bernita was shot. This only adds to the overall mystery of unanswered questions about this case. The Michigan State Police attempted several times to tell Mr. and Mrs. Sims of the dreadful news. It was several hours before troopers were able to find anyone at home.

According to police reports, on June 23, 2001, Trooper Crawford of the Michigan State Police Detroit Freeway Post arrived at the home address to inform Bernita's parents of the tragic news concerning their daughter. Mrs. Sims, who was the only one home at the time, allowed Trooper Crawford inside. When Trooper Crawford told her of the sorrowful news, she passed away of a heart attack.

The warm, always caring nurturing mother who kept the Sims family together and her daughter, my wife of eleven years, passed away within hours of each other.

NOW what do you tell the kids?

CHAPTER THREE

"A fox should not be of the jury at a gooses trial."
— Thomas Fuller

"Don't use others' prejudices as excuses for not achieving your goals; their prejudices are all the more reason for you to succeed." This is something I heard my father say many times.

I was raised by my parents to respect and treat others favorably, even if I didn't like them or disagreed with them. Many people dislike others without knowing anything about them or because of the color of their skin or because they speak a different language, or have a different religion or physical appearance. In doing so, they consider themselves superior.

I remember a story my mother told me about the color of her skin. My mother, Mary, is a very light skinned woman. Her mother Estelle, who was Cherokee Indian, married a Black man, Gene Dula. My mother told me that when she was little, people treated her differently by virtue of her lighter skin and hair color. My grandmother would comb brewed coffee through my mother's hair to make her hair darker. That was 70 years ago. Not much has changed today.

People continue to draw conclusions based on what they perceive. Throughout the investigation of the death of my wife, I have been created in the minds of others as a cold-blooded killer, a womanizer, an intelligent, plot planning, narcissistic psychotic.

Although a reply to any of these allegations doesn't warrant a response, it does need to be addressed. It's easy to fall into the mob mentality surrounding this case because of the mystery and the time it has taken to resolve. But, if you look at this case—more specifically the investigators involved—you will discover that the attitudes and behaviors exhibited were an attempt to camouflage mediocrity and the doubts investigators had about their feelings of superiority.

At first blush, you will find the investigators to be ill informed. If I choose to acknowledge their comments, (and sometimes it is best not to) it is only to educate them and leave them with something profound to think about. I have concluded that they have the problem; I don't. It is more important for me to keep my eye on the goals I have created than to fall to the pressures of others' inadequacies and shortcomings.

Seventy years ago, the best solution was to cover the differences with brewed coffee. Today, education is obtained by the printed word. My mother who is 75 today has had to deal with differences all of her life. What I have learned from her is life is not always fair but then again who said it would be?

My mother is a strong lady and has been through many more of life's mishaps than I may ever experience. She lost my father to cancer several years ago, but has never allowed that to pull our family down. She suffered from the leeches and jackals that preyed on her for our farm equipment when my father died. It was not a pleasant experience to watch my mother endure, but I am a stronger person because she demonstrated such determination to sew our family back together.

Everyone suffers many disappointments, heartaches, letdowns, and setbacks. That's just the way it is. It is very easy to look at others' prosperity and complain about what an unfair hand you were dealt. This is the life we have there's no returning it for another. Complaining doesn't help and neither does wallowing in self-pity. Whatever hand you are dealt, you still are given the opportunity to play it to the best of your ability. The fact is if I don't try to play this hand, I'll never have the opportunity to see this case resolved.

"That's a piece of Art," my father said with his playful attitude when I was born. Could you blame him? He waited so long for a son after three girls. My father was a complete jokester. I get a lot of that from him. Everybody loved my father. I have big shoes to fill in that category. He always treated everyone fairly because even though he was raised through some unfair times he knew the importance of instilling the right thing into his kids.

"Be the same as you are in public and in private," my father once told me. "People will remember how well you treated them years later but may forget your name tomorrow."

I don't remember when my father started placing goodies in my shoes after he had worked all night into the next day. Everyday I would wake up and dash downstairs to see what my father left for me. Everyday, without fail, I would find a little treat in my shoe. Sometimes I would plant a few extra shoes to solicit more goodies and for the most part, I would get them. Little did I know then that was my father's snack from his lunch. He would save his snack for me because I looked forward to the mystery of what could be in that shoe. That was a special event for me and me only because I was the youngest; certain privileges come with certain gifts. My mother was not the only one teaching life lessons in our family.

If there was a perfect combination of my mother and my father, that would be my oldest sister, Angela. Angela is from the old school, naturally because she is the oldest. The first of three girls and two boys, Angela had to play many roles including caretaker of four younger siblings. Maybe that's why she's into management today. Angela is nobody to mess with.

Angela doesn't take crap from any one. I think she's always spring loaded to the kick butt position. Family trauma is an effective way to gauge how a family works under pressure. Angela never once blinked during the recuperation of this incident.

The police never talked to Angela about our relationship or mine with Bernita. Angela lives in New Jersey. And although she was willing to be interviewed and even went so far as to call the New Jersey State Police to give them her availability. No one called.

My sister Karen is the toughest, meanest person in our family. "The enforcer," Karen is the type of person who would physically harm anyone who might muster up the courage to mess with this family. Underneath that tough persona lies the most caring heart you could imagine. Karen is streetwise. She has good street sense but very few people know her sweet side. The protector stood guard that week of June 23, 2001. After falling apart at the thought of someone wanting to kill her sister-in-law, Karen dug down deep in her soul and was ready to guard the family once again.

Arlyce is my youngest sister: bright, quick thinking, cunning and mean. Did I say mean before? Must be a family trait. Arlyce is all business. Always has been. I remember working on our farm, picking cotton on our knees with the hot sun bearing down on us like a machine press. The cotton mill would give us a smattering three cents per pound for picked cotton. The average person on an average day could pick 80 pounds. You don't have to do the math to learn that makes for a long day with short pay.

In the middle of one day, Arlyce stood up and announced she wasn't going to pick cotton anymore. My grandmother, Daisy Bell White, shouted for her to return to the fields. Arlyce calmly said, "I'll get a job and pay you enough for me NOT to pick cotton." She has always been all business. This incident was tough on her because she could foresee the damage it would cause. She is a professional woman and she knows the inner workings of business and politics. Arlyce's biggest struggle is with lawyers and police departments. Their seemingly uncaring attitudes do not fit well with her opinions.

Mark at thirty-six is the baby in the family. Mark has a no-nonsense attitude to everything in life. He has a very simple approach supported by personal belief and sheer simple logic. That's a trait I need to learn from him. After Mark speaks, you never have to guess what he was trying to say. He is very blunt, direct and to the point. This incident has drawn us closer together. Good results, wrong reason. He is good at not allowing simple things to bother him, a quality that all of us should share.

My family says they have newfound respect for me because I am doing so well raising my daughters alone. I don't think that is such a large task. It comes natural, but you do have to place your life on the back burner to give your children all the attention and nurturing they need.

My entire family was very supportive throughout the entire incident. Nephews and nieces, cousins, aunts and uncles have all shared their support, thoughts and feelings. The surprise support person, who has been referred to as "The Glue," is Dr. Mia Piggee, my niece. She is mother to my nephew and namesake, Zane Artis Piggee. (You have to just love his middle name!)

Mia has come through time and time again totally ignoring her professional and personal life to make sure Uncle and his family will make it through this. Some of her tenacious caring and genuine concern is inherited from her mother, Angela, but more of it has to do with the fact she is a doctor and a natural caregiver. Everyone in this family had something to contribute to ease my family's pain during this tragedy. Mia glued it all together.

CHAPTER FOUR

"Two things are bad for the heart—running up stairs and running down people."

—Bernard M. Baruch

As I remember, it was a day in the summertime in June of 1986. I had decided that MSP was for me. I was in the process of keeping a good driving record so I could enter *any* police department. I didn't need any more tickets or any mishaps with the police because of my driving record.

On that day in June, I was driving on the John C. Lodge freeway in Detroit, Michigan with a very old looking 1976 Dodge Cordoba, which was on its last leg. The vehicle didn't have the proper registration plates on it. I would venture to confess that it probably didn't have the proper insurance either. The vehicle had a mechanical problem, a loud exhaust. So, as chance would have it, a state trooper pulled me over because the exhaust on the vehicle was too loud. Of course, my expectation as to how state police should present themselves was very high.

The trooper who stopped me on that day was severely overweight, appearing as though he was in his third trimester. He even had trouble exiting his vehicle as he labored up towards my car. Now comes the old familiar "How are you today?"

"How fast do you think you were going?" he started the conversation with me.

I believe my reply was the standard, "I believe I was going along with the flow of traffic."

"I need to see your driver's license, proof of insurance and registration please."

At that point, I felt I should be honest with the rotund officer and so I explained to him why I would not be able to find my insurance and that I was going to try and get the exhaust fixed as soon as I could. I did let him know it was my goal and mission in life to become a state trooper just like him. He asked me whose registration plates were on the vehicle. I told him I was borrowing the plates from a friend of mine.

He said, "You know I could take you to jail right now, don't you?"

I said, "Yes, sir, of course I know you can."

He went back to his car for what seemed like an eternity of lifetimes. He returned with three tickets in his hand. That day I received a ticket for no proof of insurance, improper registration and loud exhaust. I promptly paid the fines for the violations because I was guilty.

The citations delayed my application two years. But, what shocked me most about that officer was as he was going back to his car he said, "By the way you don't want to be me." And he walked away. He got in his vehicle and drove off as I sat there on the expressway trying to figure out how the heck he made it.

The way we perceive police differs greatly now from the way we perceived police twenty years ago. Probably my biggest influence for becoming an officer with the state police came from a retired trooper whose name I can't even remember, and will probably never see again. I don't have anyone who is a police officer in my family. Prior to applying, I didn't even know anyone who was a police officer. This trooper, when I came to Lansing for my second interview, was walking along the side of the post picking small pieces of trash off the lawn. What he was doing was actually cleaning the lawn, to allow his post to be more professional.

He was dressed in full uniform, walking along the side of the post picking up small pieces of paper. "What pride!" I thought to myself. I was so impressed that I couldn't wait for my bad driving record to clear.

It wasn't until twelve years later that I learned that trooper had severe alcohol related problems and was repeatedly reprimanded for alcohol related violations. Ironically, he assisted with my background investigation. He even commented to employment contacts during my background investigation how strange it was that I had never consumed alcohol.

During the latter stages of my background investigation, he interrogated me about the subject of alcohol. He thought I was lying. "Everybody has had at least one drink sometime or another." He told me. "You aren't one of these Jesus freaks are you?"

I felt like taking a swig just to get him off my back. Prior to my coming into the department, I looked upon him as a symbol of what a Michigan State Police Officer should be.

To me and I believe for the reader of this book, it is important to know the perceptions of police and their police departments vary greatly from one community to another. Given that, it is important to know that the duty of police officers and their obligation to serve the public with integrity and competence has nothing to do with public opinion. Nevertheless, almost every police department, if not every police department, experiences its share of problems, especially ethical problems.

A police department exempt from any type of internal control that succumbs to the pressure of political influence and even public opinion will at some juncture lose the admiration of the public and will become incompetent and flawed.

It is a thin blue line that we police officers walk every day as an avenue to serve the public under the rule of law.

WHO KILLED MY WIFE?

But, we become unjust and fail greatly when we attempt to serve the public only to satisfy the multitude of perceptions from the public. As a police officer, it is a privilege to be able to serve in our democratic society. A system of government for the people by the people cannot happen without the assistance of the police because we as police officers have such a profound affect on how people conduct their lives. We have a huge responsibility and that responsibility should only be entrusted to people of good character, to people who make good moral decisions.

I was armed with good moral ethics, good moral fiber, and an excellent upbringing. The will and desire to become a police officer isn't enough. When I applied to become a police officer, I was the same as hundreds and hundreds of others vying for so few positions. The first several interviews did not go well. I was not offered a job until I spoke with a good friend of mine, Richard Battle. He asked how well I was interviewing. I told him the interview panel always asked, "Why do you want the job?" My reply was always the same — so I could help people. Richard told me that wasn't what the Human Resources Department within any police agency wants to hear because now they know that it is a lie.

People do not want to become a police officer just to help people. People want to become police officers so they can do a good job, make money and draw a good retirement. As soon as I said I wanted the job for that reason, I was offered a job with the state police right away.

I have been with the Michigan State Police for over fourteen years. I have been a detective sergeant for over eight years with the agency. Within that span of time, I have had several different jobs to include recruiting, organized crime, criminal investigation unit, diversion investigation unit, technical services and private security and investigations unit. I was quickly promoted to sergeant with only five and a half years of MSP employment. I was class orator of my recruit class. I was even Criminal Investigation Division's Trooper of the Year in 1998.

The knack for investigations is fairly easy and natural for me. It has never been a task for me to conduct any type of investigation. I have a good feel for police work and investigations. I have made a lot of accomplishments and I have received a lot of training within the department, on my own, and prior to becoming a state trooper.

I will say, and this statement is difficult because police work is my livelihood, as a police officer you possess powers that no one else has and you have unlimited discretion in using those powers. But police officers candidly are often not professionals. We work in a profession that is unprofessional. There is no regulation or requirement for a police department to conduct itself as a professional organization. The reason I say this is because there is no support structure for police departments. Each police department is built on its own structure. When that structure begins to deteriorate whether it be one brick at a time, or all at once, it is up to the individual police department to replace that brick or ignore the structure until the whole foundation comes tumbling down. This allows for fragmented mini systems within police departments to the point that they sometimes don't even have the capability of communicating with each other.

Speaking of perceptions, one perceived notion from the public is that every police officer is the same and there exists one big net system in which all the police officers operate as one whole unit. This simply is not true. A department sometimes motivated by irrational management decisions, political influences, and unmotivated police officers will succumb to the pressures of the public. The opportunities of promotion, departmental recognition and the ever-prevalent selected enforcement soon become career goals.

If a police department doesn't have a solid foundation and there is the possibility of outside political influence, there may be an opportunity for personal gain. This creates a very, very dangerous unstoppable highly motivated and politically influenced machine.

In this book, I maintain that the investigators assigned to this case are motivated by poor management, weak leadership, and ineffective investigative agendas. Because of this, I also maintain and conclude that this investigation has stalled and/or never proceeded forward from the first forty-eight hours due to the result of all of the above.

In the final analysis, the bottom line is that the investigators broke their oath of office. They deprived Bernita of any possibility of finding her killer. The investigators individually, if not as a group, have failed in their efforts for the simple reason that they did not withdraw from this case when faced with their inadequacies. They ought to have been required to withdraw considering their personal shortcomings.

The first mistake in this case was the assignment of the officers. Investigators who knew me (some who were friends of mine) were assigned to this case. That is one of the biggest rules in police work. An officer can never give a sound or just opinion nor conduct a proper investigation against someone he/she knows. I would argue that there shouldn't have been any investigators assigned at all, to investigate **my** background other than to quickly eliminate me as a suspect.

Several not only knew me but had worked for me or with me. This doesn't allow for a neutral investigation, one way or another. If a detective knows or works with the suspect, he cannot render an impartial judgment one-way or the other, whether he likes that person or does not like that person. It is impossible for a person who knows me not to make personal judgments for or against me in this case.

My example is Detective Sergeant Mary Treat. Not only did I supervise her, but also up until this investigation, we were good friends. Detective Sergeant Sam Hornberg is another example. Prior to this investigation, I considered him a friend. He is no longer. I have worked on several cases with both of these detectives. The normal approach is to assign investigators outside the area of my regular responsibilities. It would have been proper and much more effective for the state police to bring detectives from the northern areas of Michigan. Within the Lansing Police Department (LPD) many investigators know me. I am an investigator myself. It is the circle I keep.

Another lethal error that was made deals with jurisdiction. The area where Bernita was shot and killed is a public area within the city of Lansing. Because I am an employee of the state police, MSP offered their assistance with the investigation. There was an internal struggle between the Michigan State Police and the Lansing Police Department about jurisdiction and whose case it was. One rationale for the state police to become involved in the case is because of my civil lawsuit against the state police. Prior to Bernita's death, my lawyers filed a civil suit on my behalf. I cannot comment about the lawsuit because it is pending but it is important to know that the lawsuit was filed prior to Bernita's death. I mention this because it is interesting enough as the Lansing Police Department was conducting interviews; the state police were conducting their own interviews by asking civil questions under the guise of the homicide investigation.

Several of the witnesses that I have talked to and/or surveyed have said they were asked numerous times in several different interviews about the civil litigation. This is a rare opportunity for an employer to have the right to investigate an employee who is filing a lawsuit. Time was severely wasted by state police investigators because they asked questions concerning the civil litigation.

This type of questioning made the witnesses uncomfortable and ultimately confused people as to the focus of the investigation. I would like to point out that the civil case and the murder cannot in any way be related. However, the state police were allowed to gain information to forward to the attorney general's office to use in their defense in my civil case.

I mentioned before there was a problem with jurisdiction. LPD said they were in charge. MSP said it was their case. Without the proper structure within both departments and because the two departments were 'dueling' for exclusive autonomy the investigation was severely hampered. There was so much emphasis placed on who should be in charge and no emphasis was placed on who should solve the crime. Something that every investigator knows is the basic fact that if you do not locate the perpetrator within the first forty-eight hours your chance of ever locating the violator diminishes by 90 percent. These crucial forty-eight hours were wasted on bickering between the departments, lack of departmental structure and overall inexperience within the LPD detective division. This severely reduced the chances of finding Bernita's real murderer.

LPD assigned investigators to this case who were not highly motivated or experienced. At this juncture, I am merely paraphrasing what I have heard others say about LPD detectives. Currently, LPD's detective bureau is made up of officers who are there on rotating duty.

The old timers and 'salts' (I have talked to several) have moved on. They have taken valuable street knowledge and education with them. The bureau now has inexperienced officers in a rotating position. This problem is so much of a concern that LPD Chief Matt Alloy hired a private investigator to investigate this case.

In today's detective cases, knowledge is power, but knowledge is limited by personal experiences. I probably could not interview another police officer for this type of crime for lack of experience. Then again, police officers can always withdraw. I would not have accepted this case.

There is no way anyone can possibly know everything, but it is easy for us to feel self-righteous and believe we are correct in believing others have done wrong. It is also easy to harbor negative feelings about someone just because they are different than you. I will say that I am a different person than LPD is used to dealing with. Police investigators can dislike or even hate other people without knowing anything about them based solely on how they act, how they appear, what police department they work with, their type of language, race religion or anything. This stereotyping is very destructive and added to the difficulties in solving this case.

Stereotyping by LPD is not a thing of the past. It is alive and well today categorized now with different terminology.

Yesterday it was stereotyping. Today it is profiling. Allow me to say this. Police departments will profile. It's as simple as that. Whether an officer makes a profile stop on you because you are Black, White, male or female you can and will get profiled. Whether or not any type of enforcement action will be taken against you may be determined by your race. That's why police department's reports on profile stops are lopsided because they only reflect how many Black, White Hispanic, etc. citizens were stopped for a traffic violation. The reports do not accurately reflect if a citizen was asked to have his vehicle searched, given a ticket, forced to pay a higher penalty, etc. as a result of his skin color. That discretion is left up to the individual officer in control.

Police are granted discretion because no set of laws and regulations can prescribe what to do in every situation. A person accepting a position as a police officer must take on the task of a new obligation and live up to a higher standard. It follows that people who bear the public trust should be judged and punished by the rules retained for those who must adhere to a higher standard. Naturally, police should be judged by a higher standard because (we) have a higher impact on people's lives.

Emotional involvement in a case can only lead to negative feedback if the case does not go the way desired. When a police officer feels that the investigation is not going in a positive direction for him, he is faced with a difficult decision. He can either accept the responsibility of a stalled case, or fabricate evidence and forfeit all honesty and integrity. Police officers are not trained to retreat. Most officers only know how to forge ahead. Unfortunately, when the case stalls the investigator has nowhere to go. This is a moral judgment call; suffer the public scrutiny of an unsolved case or "fudge" a little to bring the case to fruition.

Those who enforce the law are required to follow it. When an officer uses immoral or illegal methods of obtaining information, he is wrong, no matter what the end cause may be. Illegally obtained evidence is not admissible but can be useful to the wayward officer. These tactics can be used to locate information that is irrelevant but helpful to embarrass a witness or retaliate against a suspect.

CHAPTER FIVE

"You can't legislate intelligence and common sense into people."   — Will Rogers

My first introduction to the power of police discretion came when I was a young MSP trooper working at the State Police Post in Lansing, Michigan. It was July 4, 1990. Bernita and I had been married almost a year. She was a prosperous System Engineer at Electronic Data Systems (EDS) and I was a scrapping young trooper with MSP. We decided to go to the fireworks in the City of Lansing. Tagging along with us that day was my good friend, Trooper Harris Edwards, and his lovely wife, Kim. Neither of our families had any children at the time.

We met Troopers Regina Gore and Cheri Hoffman from the Lansing MSP post downtown for the festivities. We had a wonderful time even though it was very hot that day, in the 90's I recall. I remember sitting motionless with sweat beads rolling off my forehead. After ending the day with

WHO KILLED MY WIFE?

Lansing's usual great fireworks display we headed out of town west bound on Oakland Street. It was late in the evening and traffic was bumper to bumper on our way back towards our home in Delta Township. The heat index was high as well as the temper of the drivers. We took comfort in driving an Austin Rover 1988 Sterling that Bernita purchased before we were married.

The Sterling was considered a luxury vehicle even though it came complete with numerous gremlins and was an electrical nightmare. At least the vehicle had air-conditioning. That was all we were concerned with. The Austin Sterling is a smaller vehicle designed to transport four people comfortably.

It probably was all the better that the weather was hot that day. We had the windows rolled up. I was driving. I saw a flash of light, heard a loud bang outside my window, and realized that someone had thrown a firecracker at the car. It hit the windshield damaging the wiper. I looked to my left and noticed a carload full of young people who were laughing. The driver made a sharp left turn to make his getaway. The traffic was so congested, when the driver turned left, he was trapped in the traffic.

I looked over at my good friend Harris and said, "What do you think?" Harris was then and is now a life long friend. He already knew what I was thinking. So what did we do? What any two young troopers would do. We got out of the car and went over to the trapped vehicle. I identified myself with my departmental badge and ID. Harris identified himself, too.

I asked the driver of the other car, "Why did you throw a firecracker at my car?"

"I didn't know you were a police officer," he said.

"What difference does that make?"

"We didn't mean any harm by it. We were just having fun."

"Well, it's against the law. Plus, you broke my windshield wiper blade. I'm going to arrest you later when the prosecutor approves my warrant. I need to see your driver's license."

"Why?"

"Because I want to be able to identify you later. Or I can take you to jail now."

He gave me his license and we returned to the Sterling and drove home. The next day, I talked with Trooper David Service, an old salt who was the court officer at the Lansing State Police post. I double-checked with Dave to make sure I was following proper procedure. I also received an estimate to have my windshield wiper repaired at Capitol Cadillac. Weeks went past and I did not hear anything from the Ingham County Prosecutor's office. Finally, a warrant request was authorized for the arrest of the perpetrator.

To play a neutral role from that point, I decided to

remove myself from the arrest. The suspect was arrested by MSP Lansing troopers and several weeks passed.

Curiously, I asked Sgt. John Parker why my arrest was taking so long. He left and returned from First Lieutenant Robert Power's office in a matter of minutes. I could tell there was a problem from the look on his face. "You need to see the old man," he said.

I walked in for a visit with "The Old Man" a title we used to describe the Lieutenant at the Post. I rendered a proper hand salute as required within our paramilitary structure. "Have a seat, Artis." (That usually doesn't mean you will be sipping tea with the big boss.) "Artis, there's a Lansing police officer who says there is a problem with your report," he said bluntly.

"What kind of problem?" I asked.

"He says that you and Harris robbed two guys of $250 at gunpoint."

"Who is the officer and why would he say that?"

"His name is Gene Sella and he's investigating the case."

I didn't know what to think. Here's this City officer who wasn't even a sergeant and he's investigating MY case? What about this $250? I believe it was my silence and disbelief that made the Lieutenant decide to fill the void.

"The complainant decided not to press charges for the armed robbery but he's upset you took his license," he said.

" I mailed it back to him. I needed to be able to contact him later," I told him.

Even though as state police officers Harris and I were authorized to make an arrest for felonies and misdemeanors committed in our presence anywhere in the state of Michigan, we were not necessarily prepared to do so, i.e. we didn't have a ticket book, handcuffs, gun. Not every trooper carries his primary weapon when off duty. In cases like ours, it is proper to gather information and ask for a warrant from the prosecutor's office.

I soon learned that Sella forwarded the results of his investigation to MSP Internal Affairs and Tri-County Metro Narcotics. Prior to this discovery, a meeting was held with Detective Sella, Lt. Jack Warder (Assistant Post Commander at the Lansing post), the assistant prosecuting attorney and me. The results of that meeting were not positive. Gene Sella stated he interviewed several witnesses present during the traffic stop of the suspects. He said that witnesses saw a known drug user exit the Sterling and walk to his residence. In other words, we dropped the drug dealer off. This known drug dealer said he personally knew both Harris and me from "hanging out" at the Black and Tan, a Lansing nightclub frequented by local Black people. Sella and the assistant prosecutor dismissed charges against the suspect because of "problems with my report."

The problem was I had not included the fifth person in my vehicle in my report. Further, because the fifth person was a known drug dealer, my entire report was flawed. Most importantly, Sella and the Ingham County Assistant Prosecutor dismissed the charges while Sella investigated Harris, me, and this imaginary drug dealer. I was furious. This was the first time for both Harris and me to experience the "Blue Code of Justice."

Was Sella really concerned for the good reputation of MSP? I say no. Was Sella concerned that MSP troopers were on his 'grounds' making off duty arrests? I say yes. Did Sella fabricate information to support claims from a suspect (whom by the way recanted the armed robbery claim) to solidify his bogus investigation? Absolutely. As this true story unfolds, this explanation is crucial to describe why Bernita's case has stalled. At the time of Sella's closing statement, it was my turn to speak.

"Why didn't you interview anyone in my car to find out if we gave anyone a ride?"

"Because you would all have your stories together," he said without hesitation.

"What do you mean? And those guys didn't?" I interrupted. "The Sterling won't even hold five comfortably. Where was this guy supposed to sit? On my wife's lap?"

I kept going with "Why didn't you interview Regina Gore or Cheri Hoffman? **They** are White. Maybe you would believe them." I said that to get a rise out of him, but I didn't get one. "Why do you believe I'm living beyond my means driving this

Sterling? It's Bernita's car and she's making payments just like anyone else. Didn't run the plate and do a credit check huh?"

That didn't get a rise either but I know the point got across because I took very good notes that day. I still have them. The fact remained. The suspect got away, I paid to have my windshield wiper fixed, and there's a LPD officer who believes I'm running drugs while he is playing the role of Sir Gallahad to save MSP's very own reputation. I didn't know it then, but that was a prime display of perceived notions and personal beliefs and how they can affect the outcome of another person's life. Regardless of whether or not it happened the way Sella said it did (and I promise you it did not!) was that a reason to dismiss charges made by an officer of another agency?

Because of Sella's personal beliefs, along with the power invested in him as a police officer, he was allowed to temporarily ruin the life and career of two upstanding state police troopers; regardless of what color they were. Harris and I are a pair of rare police officers. We both have never had a drink of alcohol, never smoked, never used drugs and don't use foul language. We have never been to the Black and Tan, don't personally know any drug users or dealers and have never had more than four people in an Austin Rover Sterling.

Gene Sella was in a bind. He made a mistake and could not back away from it because he did not know how to retreat. He was never trained that way. Every other police officer I ran into from LPD thought it was a joke. Tri-County Metro Narcotics members were on the lookout for me driving my Sterling.

LPD sergeant and good friend Scott Shulkey told me about the notice to look for my vehicle in any known drug-infested area. The notice was pinned up on the TCM board. Shulkey has known me for years and was surprised by what Sella was putting me through.

"He's a good officer," Shulkey told me while working out at Gold's Gym.

"I know he is but good officers make mistakes," I said. "I make mistakes. We have to embrace our mistakes, not run from them. There comes a time when you have to admit you are wrong."

One day I gave LPD Lt. Webster a ride home in my Sterling while his vehicle was in for repair. I told him to tell Sella he went for a ride in it. I later asked 'Webby' (that's what everyone calls him), "What did Sella say when you told him you rode with me in my Sterling?"

"Nothing," Webby said. "He just looked at me real funny like."

Any chance I got to nick at Sella I would take it. It's therapy because you really can't clean your reputation when a police officer ruins it for you. There's nothing else you can do but take your lumps.

I ran into Sella ten years after the incident. I was giving a presentation for the Michigan Association of Private Investigators. He was then and still is working as a private investigator for Don Cooks (MSP retired), a well-known private investigator in Lansing, Michigan. Gene approached me and apologized for the incident. I was shocked beyond belief. He said he made a mistake. I was shocked beyond compare. He said his superiors gave him his directions. I believe he meant it. With tears in his eyes he offered to buy me a drink.

I said, "Gene, you know I don't drink."

"Well, let me buy you a coke then."

He was so insistent that I let him do it. Maybe it cleansed his soul because he seemed relieved by it. Even though he was wrong, I forgive him. Not because I am a Christian but because I know how police management can place stress on an officer. Most of a police officer's stress doesn't come from the drunk you wrestle with on the street. It comes from dealing with your supervisors and the endless stream of reports you have to write. I forgave him, but he is still a coward. As a police officer, you always have the right to withdraw. You always have a choice, not accepting that choice is reflective of a coward. All human beings are responsible. All human beings cannot be trusted to behave well unless they are held accountable.

Cowards betray their responsibilities and forsake other people because they are worried about their own survival. They do not accept their responsibilities because they fear the consequences. The fact that Sella suffered more by not facing his wrongdoings eleven years ago is enough punishment in itself. I won't say we are even, but it's not my intention to seek revenge.

CHAPTER SIX

"The remedy for wrongs is to forget them."
— Publilius Syrus

As I write this book, it is very difficult because there is only one victim, one real victim who paid the ultimate sacrifice. The sacrifice of her life. It is laborious for me because I feel like the victim. Now that I am over the shock of my being considered a suspect, it hurts me more to know that she is gone. The little pile of dirt she swept in the corner of the bedroom is still there. She never had a chance to finish cleaning it up. The music club continues to send music, but she will never play another song. She will never know how much her daughters miss her because they aren't able to tell her.

Once the anger leaves you can feel grief. There is no relief from grief. It is the nightmare that goes on and on. After many years as a detective, I admit I am still confused. Of all the interviews, surveys, meetings and police reports, nothing has revealed any clue as to what Bernita may have done to deserve this ending. She did nothing but desired to spend time with her daughters. What's wrong with spending time with your daughters?

Investigators should spend more time trying to solve the case and less time trying to prove that I did it. They are like ping-pong balls in a wind tunnel; bouncing off shallow clues landing on empty ended leads. The motive? The pending divorce.

Bernita and I were involved in the initial stages of a divorce. We had both agreed to live our lives separately and raise our two children together. The divorce was going along amicably. We lived in the same house, went to church together, attended functions together, peacefully. We tried to carry on normal conversations because we felt it was important for the children to realize the divorce was not their fault. The children knew about the divorce because we sat them down and explained everything to them. We did not want Alanna and Michala to feel that their home was in shambles because we had decided to live separate lives.

The police and media over-emphasized the divorce. They tried to make it seem as if we were going through a vicious divorce and that Bernita was in fear for her life. This simply is not true. If this were the case, she would have packed her bags, moved out, and obtained a restraining order.

Bernita was not killed by someone she knew. She just did not live the type of life where someone would want to harm her. I have known her for a long time. Fifteen years is a long time to get to know someone. Some things slip through the cracks but there would have been more hints or clues that would suggest she was mixing with the wrong crowd. There is no evidence of that. The motive of a pending divorce is weak. Even if a divorce is of a violent nature, that standing alone is not motive enough to try to build a case around. Motive makes movies and sitcoms. Evidence and facts jail people. Anything short of that is a prosecutor's nightmare and the beginnings of a bad, B-rated movie. Since current images of police are drawn largely from television programs with no semblance to reality, public expectations are not realistic. Investigators in this case did not know their mission and they are not dedicated. The public regards them as trustworthy agents serving in their role for the goodness of mankind. The investigators, both LPD and MSP should be determined to deserve the confidence and trust of the public, not merely to appear to be worthy. If these detectives are worried about public perceptions, I can guarantee they will trick the public by covering up mistakes rather than by improving their practices. The Police are supposed to serve the public, not gratify a sitcom-type perception. The pending divorce motive is a lousy excuse for not doing a good job.

CHAPTER SEVEN

"Excess of grief for the deceased is mindless; for it is
an injury to the living and the dead know it not."
— Xenophon

June 23, 2001. It was a sunny day that started around
5:30 a.m. I had a chance to sleep in. Normally, I wake up at 5
a.m. with or without an alarm clock. I've been caught in that
internal system for years. The morning started quietly enough
until our dog, Chili, a hyperactive, out of control Yellow Lab
who was just a year then, escaped through our backyard fence
and into the wild blue yonder. I had let him out for his morning
stretch and gone to get his food and water. When I called Chili
he didn't come. He was nowhere to be seen. Trouble first thing,
I thought—how I wish that were our only trouble that day.

That was the first time he had run away. I didn't know
what to expect but I knew the girls would be worried and
very unhappy.

"Alanna, Chili got out. I'm going to go see if I can find
him," I said.

"Where did he go?"

"I don't know. I don't see him outside anywhere."

"Can I come?" She always wants to go everywhere with me.

"Why don't we hop in Mavis and see if we can find him."

Mavis was my 1986 Dodge Omni. The kids loved that car because they could sit in the front seat without worrying about injuries from an airbag. "It's my turn to sit up front!" Alanna said. Alanna is my oldest. She always creates these little rules that somehow give her the edge. I can never remember whose turn it is anyway!

"Let's see if Michala and Mom want to give us a hand and take the other car. That way we can call each other when we find him."

"Good idea Dad!"

I went looking for Bernita. She was upstairs getting ready for the day. Michala, my youngest was watching television in the family room.

"Chili got out," I told Bernita.

"What do you mean?"

"He got out of the fence some kind of way. The gate is open and I don't see him back there anywhere."

"Did you look across the street at Joe's?"

"Yeah, that's where I was all this time. I checked Joe's,

Cathi's and Beth's yards. I whistled but he never comes for that anyway. Can you and Michala take the van and Alanna and I will take Mavis? Maybe if we all look for him we might get lucky."

"I guess. What time is it?"

"I don't know. What time do we have to be at Potter Park for Rachel's party (Rachel is Michala's best friend.)?"

"Around one. Did Alanna sign the card?"

"Yeah. Grab the Nextel so we can give each other a bump if we find him."

We went off in separate directions looking for that dog. All along, Alanna was asking me what we were going to do if we didn't find him. I kept reassuring her that Chili would be found.

"Do you think he was lonely and wanted to be with other dogs?" she asked me with those big almond eyes of hers.

You can always tell when something troubles her because her eyes well up only at the corners. They were close to bursting now. "No Scoobs." That's her nickname.

"I think Chili is very happy here with us. We ain't dogs but he likes us just as well."

"Well, when he gets back, I'm going to give him a big ole' hug and a treat."

"Me, too, Scoobs. Me, too."

WHO KILLED MY WIFE?

I never lie to my daughters but I was a little worried this time. I didn't want to worry them because it hurts me so much to see them sad. That's probably why Bernita and I stayed together for as long as we did. Neither one of us wanted to hurt our kids, but we wouldn't lie to them to try to make things better.

We searched the entire neighborhood to no avail. Bernita decided to break it off first and take Michala home. On the way back, Alanna and I stopped a jogger and asked if she had seen our dog, but we didn't have any luck. I gave the description of Chili to our mail carrier in case she came across him.

"Hey, Dad."

"Yeah, Scoobs."

"You think we can make some posters with Chili's picture on it?"

"Yeah, sweetie. We can do that when we get home."

Colin, our ten-year-old neighbor, met us when we got home. He volunteered to take his bike as far as his parents would let him to look for Chili. We live in a caring neighborhood and help each other whenever we can.

When I walked in the door there was a message on our answering machine. Chili was found! He had climbed over hill and dale, across four lanes of traffic, through the woods and come to rest about two miles away. He was in the safety of a kind, young woman and her six dogs. Maybe Alanna was right. Chili did want to be with other dogs. No, that wasn't it. He just wanted to make sure he was missed. It worked because nobody wanted to lose him.

We headed out for Rachel's party slightly after 12:30 p.m. Rachel's parents were having her birthday party at the pavilion in Potter Park. This party was an event that Michala did not want to miss. Alanna was not interested in going to Rachael's birthday party because she wanted to go to her friend, Chelsea's party at Delta Mills Park in Delta Township. We decided to go to Delta Mills first because it was closest. Bernita drove our 2000 Honda Odyssey van. It was unusual that she drove that day. She drove the Honda van everyday to work. That was her vehicle but whenever we were together, I always drove.

I can count the number of times she drove with me in a vehicle on my right hand with two fingers and a thumb missing. When we arrived at Delta Mills Park, Chelsea was flying a kite with her mother and a few other adults. I only know Chelsea's mother and father from Winans School where our children attend. They are a nice family, but I rarely have a chance to say more than a hello or goodbye when I see them.

At that point, I didn't know what was going on. Bernita and I conversed but I didn't know whom, if either of us was going to stay at Delta Mills Park and who would go with Michala to Potter Park. Alanna, my little adventurer would do anything by herself if we allowed her to. Michala, on the other hand, required at least one parent's attention during outings.

"You guys need me to stay here with the kids?" I asked the crowd of adults.

"No, looks like four parents to one kid now. Kinda got them out numbered." One of the parents replied.

Alanna was already swinging with Chelsea. I walked down the hill and gave her a kiss and hug and said goodbye. From there we left for the Potter Park Pavilion to meet Rachel. It was a very beautiful day. We arrived at the park just as Bill and his family arrived. Bill is Rachel's father. "I'll help with the food if you don't mind," I told Bill. He and I carried the food and a stroller in to the park.

I didn't know Bill or his family that well. They seemed like a nice family. I would see them as they picked up their daughter from daycare. Bill introduced me to his wife and his brother, John. Bill and his wife work for the Department of Mental Health. Bill and I compared notes, telling each other war stories about our jobs. I spent most of my time talking with Bernita and Bill and video taping our girls taking swings at the piñata. Bill tried to accelerate the process by creating a small opening in the piñata for the next would be challenger. All of us burst into laughter when Bill made the opening a little too big and all the candy burst into the air and all the children scooped it up like goldfish at the surface of a fishbowl.

There were several families at the pavilion. One Black family was present for a reunion. As we made plans to leave, a strange but pleasant surprise awaited me. MSP Detective First Lieutenant Ken Knowlton's son approached me and started talking. I had not seen him since he ran long distance track in high school. He is a spitting image of his father, Ken.

"My how time flies, " I thought as I talked with him, his wife and their two-year-old child.

Shortly after talking with Ken's son, we started packing to be on time to go back and pick up Alanna. The rest of the party was prepping for a trip through the zoo. We had no intentions of going because we had to get back to Delta Mills Park. Michala had a different agenda. She decided she wanted to go to the zoo with Rachel. She made a big production number of a temper tantrum, and in the end, it worked. Bernita said "Why don't you go get Alanna and meet us at the zoo entrance?"

I agreed. No need of to have a major temper tantrum on our hands, so I kissed Michala on the forehead, she kissed me on the elbow. Then, I packed a few items to save on trips to the van and headed over to pick up Alanna. Little did I know that would be the most important trip I've ever made according to the investigators.

It wasn't that important to me. I clearly remember the first thing I did when I got in the van after putting on my seat belt was to give my friend Mike Mshar a call. Mike is a member of the car club I belong to. He planned to come over to my house later in the early evening to pick up an auto part. I gave Mike a call but he wasn't in so, I left a message for him on his cell phone. Then, it was time to call my good friend Reginald Hoskins. I've known Reginald (Doc) ever since I was in my early twenties. Reginald was my best friend before this incident. We did everything together, shared our innermost secrets, and supported each other whenever possible. So, it was natural to give Doc a call to catch-up on some old times.

I talked to Doc from the moment I left Potter Park until I arrived at Delta Mills Park where I initially dropped off Alanna. I even spent some time talking to Doc in the parking lot before going in to pick up Alanna. When I got to the picnic site, there weren't many people around. Alanna was playing with Chelsea.

There were just a few parents there. I had a general conversation with one of the parents concerning auto insurance. Alanna and I left. As we were driving back, Alanna was telling me how much fun she had at the party.

Shortly after we left the park, Mike Mshar gave me a call to let me know what time he was coming over to my house to pick up the turbo I was planning on selling him. We negotiated a price as I explained to him how wonderfully his car would run after bolting on my turbo.

As we got closer to the park, I noticed it was becoming congested. Traffic was everywhere. When I crested the hill on Pennsylvania, I noticed the area was covered with police officers. I was still talking to Mike at the time. I told Mike it looked like there was an emergency at Potter Park and I would have to call him back. I hung up the phone as I passed Potter Park to turn left at the next available street.

"What happened?" Alanna asked

"I don't know Scoobs."

I didn't know any other way into the park except for the front entrance. I drove around to find another entrance.

"Is Mommy going to be OK?"

"Yes, Mommy is going to be OK."

I then tried to call Bernita on her cell phone. I had to leave a message because she didn't pick up the phone. "Dad?"

"Yeah, Scoobs."

"Are they going to let us in?" she asked.

"Yes, honey. We're going to go inside as soon as we find out how."

"Dad can you go home and get your uniform so they will let us in?"

I didn't answer her because I didn't even have a uniform. I have not had one for years but she always looked up to me as the super hero police officer, like the kind she sees on television. As her super hero I didn't want to let her down, so I smiled and gave her a reassuring wink. I drove around the back of Potter Park until I came to my friend, Joe Brown who works for LPD. I left Alanna in the car and went to talk to Joe. "What's going on big brother?"

"Just had a shooting," he told me.

"Really? That's why I can't get in the front. What happened?"

"Some middle-aged woman took one through the chest."

With my gallows humor I replied, "Well, I hope it's not my wife, things are rough but it's not that bad."

Police officers tend to mask their feelings to hide their emotions. That was one day I wished I never ever participated in that type of gory humor. I asked Joe if there was another way into the park because my wife and daughter were in there. I didn't want to interfere with anything LPD had going but did want to get to my family. He told me my best bet was to try to get in the front entrance. I decided to go back to the front entrance and see if LPD would at least let me know where my family was going to be dispersed. I was really beginning to worry.

On my way back to the front entrance there was a woman who was watching what was going on inside the park. I rolled down my passenger-side window and asked what was going on. She said that there had been a shooting. I tried Bernita's cell phone again but it didn't go through.

When I pulled our van over to talk to a female officer at the entrance, I knew there was a problem. I identified myself with my departmental issued identification. I told her that I worked with the state police and I wanted to know where they were letting people out. I told her that I had a wife and daughter inside. From that time on all the weight of the entire world rested inside my heart. I knew from the very exact moment this female police officer laid eyes on me, that something very terrible was going to affect me the rest of my life.

It's a strange talent, if you will, but I could tell just from the actions of everyone something very terrible had just occurred and it involved my family. The female officer said, "You need to talk to the sergeant."

Every police officer knows that when an officer raises that yellow tape to allow you entry, you are either a victim or a very important person. At the time, I didn't feel like an important person.

The officer removed the tape so that I could drive through. I pulled off to the side and we got out of the car. I told Alanna I would be right back and that I needed to go talk to the police officer. Alanna went with the female officer. When I reached the sergeant, he struggled for words to say to me. What could he possibly say? What could they possibly do? That's when the sergeant told me the horrible news. I started minimizing right away. I knew that something very awful just happened, but my first basic instinct was to deny it and then try to minimize the results. After hearing what Joe Brown told me, I knew that a middle-aged woman was involved. I tried to accept the fact that Bernita was hurt. When the sergeant told me it was a little bit more difficult to explain, I started piecing the puzzle together. I focused my mind to believe that she was critical. I looked towards the sergeant for answers. I didn't get an answer from him. He didn't know what to say. He didn't have to say anything. I knew. I knew the woman, that middle-aged woman Joe told me about, was my wife and she was dead. You can't minimize death.

There's nothing that can comfort you from that point. You don't have a chance to prepare. It's not like a sickness where you know it's going to happen. It's not like a car accident where you feel like it's somehow your fault. Even knowing it wasn't your fault, you somehow feel guilty that you could have taken a different route or just stayed home. Not here. Not this one. The only comfort I had would be in knowing the suspect was caught. I wasn't getting any confidence from the scene officers. It didn't appear that a suspect was somewhere being grilled by my brothers in Blue.

Is Michala okay? I was in shock, all alone and void of any answers. What brought me back to reality was the media zeroing in like homing pigeons. It was difficult to see them through tear-filled eyes. I very seldom cry in front of my kids, but I couldn't hold back. I asked Alanna to come over to me. I told her we had to go to the hospital to see mommy. She didn't cry. She was there to protect her Dad. I cried. I didn't stop crying that day. I was a swollen tear secreting mess, still void of any rational explanation as to what happened.

"Let's take a ride in a police car, Scoobs."

"Okay, Dad."

I left the keys to the van with the female officer. I picked up the phone. "Harris?"

"Yeah," he said.

"This is Artis. Bernita was shot. I need you to meet me at the hospital. I need Kim to pick up Michala from Rachel's house. I don't know where they live."

"Which hospital?"

I had to ask the sergeant.

"Sparrow. Can you meet us there?"

"I'm on my way."

We didn't have to say anymore. My good friend Harris didn't have to ask what happened; he didn't have to explain how sad he was; he didn't have to ask me if I was okay. All that mattered from a good friend at that time was that he was there for me when I needed him. He dropped everything and almost beat the squad car to the hospital.

The ride was quiet. There was no filler conversation. No gallows humor, no changing the subject. It's just me now and this bottled anger that needs to be redirected. I felt like a failure.

I wasn't there for her then, how can I be there for my kids now? Why isn't Alanna crying? The next cameraman I see will feel the wrath of some of this misdirected anger. This is a never-ending ride. Did we pass Sparrow?

I can remember seeing the troopers' faces as I walked into the hospital. They were afraid to make eye contact. I could tell, at least at first blush, that they felt for me. It was a sense of responsibility. I even felt like the troops were going to get to the bottom of it all and at least, for a moment, I would find some comfort, somewhere. God, I wish this was all a dream.

Here I am in the room with Alanna. The room is so small you can touch every corner, sitting still. I always hated these rooms. Nothing good ever comes out of these types of rooms. The clergy comes in or the doctor swings by. Either way, it's never good news. Not in this room. Moments later, Harris showed up.

"How's Michala?" I asked.

"She's OK. She's with Kim. She's fine."

"Is she crying?"

"A little, but she's fine. Don't worry about her. Kim has her."

"Harris, (as I leaned away from Alanna) they killed her, man. Just like that. They killed Bernita. They shot her. They shot her! They didn't give her a chance. I mean, here's this sergeant trying to tell me that she was critically wounded by a high-powered rifle. Of course she was, because it was a high-powered rifle!"

Harris put his arm around my neck and left it there.

"Why would somebody do this? Huh? They were at the zoo. The zoo! Out of hundreds of people it had to be her. Who would want to hurt her?"

"Nobody," he said, "Bernita was the sweetest person in the world. Nobody would want to hurt her."

"Then why did it happen?" I snapped back at him.

"Is it because I missed church last Sunday? Is it my job? Are the girls better off without her? No. Is this going to be with them the rest of their lives? Yes. He can't get away with this. I should have been there. I don't even have my Sig with me. I should never have left. Harris?"

"What."

"It's not like we're picking out curtains or anything. Can you take your arm off my neck?"

You see, Harris is a Six-degree Grand Master Black Belt and instructor of Go-Ti School of Combative Arts. His little reassuring hug around and about the neck area was beginning to make me feel dizzy. He never knows his own strength, but I depended on his inner strength at that time. I took a break from his python grip to give Alanna some comfort. She looked at me with those almond eyes again and cracked a trembling smile. To her, Dad's superman cape was still flapping in the wind. She knew everything was going to be fine.

It was time to call the family. I started with my sister Angela. It was time to put her to the test. I could hardly speak when I told her. I couldn't hold back the tears, even in front of Harris and Alanna.

"Angie?" I said when she answered the phone.

"Artie?"

"Yes…Bernita was shot at the park. She didn't make it."

"No, Artie, no!"

There wasn't any talk about joking with each other. There wasn't any talk about playing games. Angela knew I was serious. Angela said a prayer for the family.

" Michala and Alanna are okay but I need everyone to come here."

She stumbled for a second and started thinking out loud. "Angie I need everyone here now!"

"Okay. we'll be there."

I hung up the telephone and called Bernita's mother but nobody answered. I called again. Same result. Next, I called Kim Lyons, Bernita's best friend. Kim answered the phone and I didn't know what to say. "Kim," I said, "this is Artis." I took a deep breath because I still didn't know how to tell her. I could tell that she knew something was wrong. I felt the best way to let her know was to just come out and tell her. "Somebody shot Bernita. She's dead."

Kim let out a horrendous scream that continued even after I pulled the receiver from my ear. I tried to comfort her but she could not hear me. Harris took the phone away from me and did his best to calm Kim down. He tried to explain that he needed her to try and relax. Neither one of us was very good at telling her. Police officers just are not good at breaking bad news. I gave up calling people. It was taking too much out of me.

There was another interruption. This time it was the volunteers at the hospital. They were extremely nice. Intrusive, but nice. I recognized a volunteer helper right away. It was Julie Gibbs, the secretary at Michala and Alanna's school. She was the nicest of all of them. How she held her composure, I don't know. She knew Bernita and I know it was difficult for her. The other volunteers were eager to help. The doctor showed up for his announcement. It didn't take long for him to get to the point. Maybe he thought I could handle it as a police officer.

My blank stare was interrupted by his words, "We need you to identify the body."

▲ Scene of the crime: Potter
Park Zoo, Lansing, Michigan

◄ First surprise birthday party

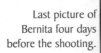

▶

Last picture of
Bernita four days
before the shooting.

At a dance together in 2000.

Before the shooting, little sister
protecting big sis.

The summer of the shooting
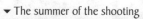

Bernita during a happier time ▶

▲ (Back Row L to R): Bernita, Tinora, Loni, Karen, Reggie with Cheyenne, Mark, Kimberly, Tracey, Mary, Angela; (Front Row L to R):Chili the dog, Artis with Michala, Alanna, Dayna, Mia, Arlyce, Anthony with Jalen.

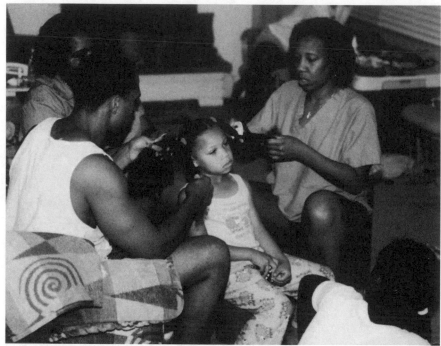

▲ Hair 101 class for Dad with the help of two experts tackling the hair of a very serious yet patient and beautiful Michala.

Now on his own, Dad has confidence to handle both Michala and Alanna's
▼ black locks which now cascade down their backs.

CHAPTER EIGHT

"How little do they see what really is; who frame their empty judgment upon that which seems."
— Robert Southey

Detective South from LPD led Harris and me to the Lansing Police Department's South Precinct. I had never met South, a young looking officer with probing eyes that were constantly searching. Maybe it was his slim frame that made him look so young. "Inch High Private Eye" I thought. I soon got the feeling that LPD didn't have any direction or focus in this case. It may have been the fact I had so much pent up frustration that time stood still. I was certain that LPD could find the perpetrator with help from me. The sooner we got this man, the sooner we could go on living our lives.

The interview team was made up of Detectives Priest and Hemmingway. I had never met either but both Priest and Hemmingway pretended they knew me from years ago. The interview was standard protocol with Priest on my left and Hemmingway on my right. Right away, I had a strange feeling. It wasn't enough that I was to be interviewed by the police for a crime I didn't commit, but there seemed to be a sense of urgency on the investigator's part. I felt as if Priest and Hemmingway had never worked together or interviewed anyone. Their approach was haphazard and unorganized.

They were trying to determine the nature of the ocean by studying a glass of water. They were not prepared. I was prepared for the night to be over. I was upset, angry and anxious to catch the guy who made my world stand still and my heart race away. The natural instinct for a person who is placed in this unfortunate predicament is to be angry. Anger is the second emotion to surface after sorrow. As a police officer and a husband, I wanted to do everything I could to catch the perpetrator. It is another basic instinct of a human being to want justice to prevail. When the tragedy is personal and close to home, the emotion takes on a vengeful stance. The fourteen-year police officer instinct within me prevailed and perpetuated a "Catch the bad guy" spirit. I wanted to do all I possibly could to find the perpetrator.

Naturally, I wanted to help the police, as anyone would. The questions from the investigators were standard and mundane. It appeared Priest and Hemmingway were stalling or waiting for something. As we sat in the interview room at LPD, I thought to myself *what is taking them so long to get to the point*? Forty-five minutes of the evening was wasted asking the same questions repeatedly. "What did you do when you left the park?" "Where did you say you went?" "Who do you know that could do something like this?" I thought these questions were just a waste of time.

Everyone understands that when a husband or wife is murdered a good place to start to look for answers is with the spouse. That was one of the reasons I tolerated the filler questions for what seemed like an eternity. Suddenly the interview changed gears to the "good cop, bad cop" routine. I still don't know who was who or which was which. Hemmingway asked me about Bernita's past boyfriends. I mentioned Paul, the one-armed person Bernita was with before she started dating me. I could not answer any questions about him because I didn't know much about him. I did mention a person by the name of Sam. Sam was Bernita's male companion before she died. I discounted Sam as the possible killer because then and to this day, I believe that no one who knew Bernita would want to kill her, not a husband or a boyfriend.

It is a fact that Bernita filed for divorce just weeks before the shooting. It is also a fact that Bernita and I had been to therapy and marriage counseling for two years since I had learned about Sam. Hence, when I told investigators that Sam didn't kill her, that was the slingshot that propelled the investigation in the wrong direction. If it were not for the investigator's infantile admiration and enthusiasm for this 'love triangle,' I would not labor on this subject or even attempt to explain about Sam.

The first mistake Priest and Hemmingway are guilty of is taking this horrible murder and turning it into a soap opera.

If this investigation were televised, it would be an interesting soap opera, but not an effective way to administer justice. This investigation, from the six hours I spent in the interview room to this day, has been based upon the interaction between Bernita, Sam, me and whomever any of us has ever had sex with. If my life were an open book (and you better believe it is now), for the record, I would exaggerate and say that I have had a relatively normal sex life. Everyone makes mistakes. I have made my share. Sometimes, those mistakes lead to divorce. Mark this and mark this well... No person Bernita, Sam, or I ever had sex with killed Bernita. That premise is a lousy excuse for poor investigative work at the onset. It is also an attempt on behalf of a baffled police department to make it seem they are looking into the matter.

Large portions of the people interviewed were interrogated for the simple reason investigators believed they had sex with me. As strange as it may appear and given all the other more feasible leads LPD could have looked into, this was the core of the investigation. Several people called me to advise Hemmingway or Priest asked them if they were having sex with me.

Some people whom I have only spoken to once or twice were asked if we had sex. This conduct of 'shocking' witnesses with the sex questions was unnecessary, unethical and rude. Hemmingway even asked my niece, Mia if we had sex.

I agree with Detective South who said, "They (Priest/ Hemmingway) never should have gone that route. They spent too much time on the questions about sex." South is a good investigator. He was promoted out of the detective unit to the rank of sergeant.

So, where do investigators go from there? Recap has a pending divorce, a boyfriend, a police officer husband, sex lives and no ties. What do you do? You take the investigation and you start over. There is nothing wrong with starting over and correcting the problem the second time. I fault LPD for not starting over with a proper investigation when all their efforts to make something from nothing went astray.

If I had been the lead investigator, I would have demanded some type of foundation beyond mere speculation that because there is a spouse, he or she must be the suspect. Theatrics, not truth, was the guiding principle in this investigation. The investigators' strategy had nothing to do with the truth. It had to do with relying on the odds that the spouse committed the crime. Those are not very good odds when a 'rush to judgment' is the gamble. This may be thought of as a conspiracy to bring any person to trial without having proper evidence.

As investigators, it was their responsibility, if they believed divorce was a legitimate motive, to gather evidence to prove that fact. Instead, they used innuendo and suggestions to fan the flames of an already tense case, creating, they hoped, enough smoke to mask the question everyone is asking, "Do you have the right person?"

It would follow that if the pending divorce was a motive, investigators would at least interview my neighbors to learn of any domestic quarrels or public disagreements. This never happened. My neighbors are still waiting to be interviewed by the police. The media thought it was important to interview at least one of my neighbors. Investigators may have realized that the divorce motive was weak at best and it was only a tactic to stall the public curiosity until something else surfaced.

Arguably, a detective committed to truth would not hide information that is relevant to the truth seeking process. Truth may be the paramount goal but it may conflict with the pressure to solve crimes in a move to regain public trust. A detective's caseload affects the truth-finding process. When the innocent is convicted or the guilty set free, is the truth irrelevant? That's why truth must be a primary goal of any investigation.

In building probable cause for a search warrant, Detective Priest extended the timeline to make it appear I had enough time to exit the park, take the shot, pick up my daughter and return. After witnesses came forward to dispute his time frame, Priest was faced with that same dilemma previously discussed. Do you accept responsibility for a stalled case, or do you fudge a little to forge ahead with retreat not an option?

When investigators learned I was not the person who shot Bernita, they erred drastically when they tried to develop some type of rationale to prove I hired someone. Once again, proving they can create a suspect and shop around for a crime. Again, I do not intend to blame the Lansing Police Department, but I do hold them accountable for not starting over when they knew I was not the perpetrator. The fact remains; I intend to continue my search for the perpetrator. However, the search is futile without the cooperation from the police department.

I understand this investigation involves prying, pursuing, and trying to discover the unknown. We permit the police to require a suspect to stand in a lineup, take samples of blood for testing, ask for handwriting samples, and fingerprints. Experienced investigators value physical evidence because we know it increases the probability of prosecuting a case. Physical evidence is so valuable that, in some cases officers may generate it themselves. Physical evidence is the strongest way to 'make' a case.

At times physical evidence isn't available and it's deemed necessary to fudge to obtain a conviction or confession. In other instances, the evidence is solid, but it's necessary to shade the truth about where it came from. This is, of course, perjury, but it happens. Perjury has two main uses: to justify an affidavit for a search warrant, and to supply probable cause. Police officers often use information obtained from 'snitches' or 'informants' in their warrant affidavits. It is not necessary to prove this information is true. You only have to suggest it is probable.

Illegally obtained evidence is not admissible. However, inadmissibility doesn't preclude its usefulness. Example, in this case, investigators used illegal methods to obtain a credit report from my sister, Arlyce and her family. They were attempting to ascertain whether or not they had used their money to help me hire a killer.

As investigators realized I was not the killer, they searched for clues that I may have hired someone to kill Bernita. After searching my bank records for large deposits and withdrawals, and finding none, investigators searched for other clues to support a hired killer theory.

A credit history report can show investigators where and what type of credit a person has applied for. The credit report can also reflect when large purchases were made. The legal way for police to obtain credit information is to subpoena the records from a person's credit reporting agency. It is more time consuming for a police officer to subpoena credit records for a resident of a different state. Judges scrutinize out state warrant and subpoena requests very closely.

Arlyce and her husband Anthony are hard working career-oriented people. They have invested their money well. As a result, they have profited from their earnings and live a very successful life. Because Arlyce and Anthony live in New Jersey, it was not convenient for Michigan investigators to request a credit report from them. Michigan investigators obtained a credit report for Arlyce and Anthony under the guise that Anthony was applying for employment as a Michigan State Trooper. It is easy to run a credit check for a possible candidate by indicating the check is for employment purposes. There is no need to seek out of state subpoenas. An investigator simply goes to a computer, keys in the information under "Employment Purposes" and prints out the information. Of course, Anthony has never applied for employment in the state of Michigan. Only because Arlyce was attempting to sell her house, did she watch her credit closely.

They took the easy way out, albeit, the illegal way out and fudged the truth. This dirty tactic would not have been discovered if Arlyce did not thoroughly read her mail. (Remember, she's the mean sister.) Is that type of conduct justifiable when an investigator is doing the best he can with what he has to get the bad guy at any cost? It is not, when it is YOUR family. Experienced investigators understand that even a weak case with fabricated evidence can still result in search warrants for the 'offender.' It is very enticing to a city police officer to try to bring down a Michigan State Police Detective Sergeant for a crime.

At some point in time, you have to move on. You may not be able to prove a person is a murderer within the time span of year or so, but you can clear that same person in a matter of days or weeks. Investigators refused to talk to people who could positively prove my innocence. They ignored eyewitnesses who could confirm my whereabouts until weeks after the crime. That information was not on their agenda. The fact is investigators did not want any information that could possibly clear me, from the very beginning.

For example, they never chemically tested my hands for gunpowder residue. They never asked for my shirt for the same purpose, but I gave it to them after I asked if they wanted it.

They did ask for my shoes, which I voluntarily gave to them. They wanted consent to search Bernita's van, which I drove and my home computer. I gave them our cell phones but they gave them back because they didn't want them. They did subpoena the phones later.

Hemmingway asked if I owned a long gun, to which I replied I did not. I even asked if he wanted to come to my house to search for it but he refused. All they wanted was the van and my computer. They kept the van for six months and returned the computer after one year. The computer was totally inoperable and void of warranty.

All through the interview, Priest and Hemmingway attempted to coerce me into a confession. Frankly, they never offered anything that would make a guilty person confess, so as an innocent person, I only found them annoying. Precious time was wasting away and they were steadily asking me to give them reasons why I didn't do it. A guilty person has to make excuses as to why he didn't commit the crime. An innocent person doesn't have to. The innocent person's explanation is elementary; he didn't because he didn't do it. Period. That was basic information both Priest and Hemmingway chose to ignore. Possibly the most disturbing confession tactic they used was to appeal to my emotions.

WHO KILLED MY WIFE?

Detective Priest was responsible for obtaining the search warrants for my vehicle, work office, Bernita's place of employment and our home. A police officer can swear to the facts of a search warrant when he has probable cause or a reason to believe a search of a person, place or thing may reveal evidence relevant to the case. A police officer must list these reasons in an affidavit and swear they are true in front of a magistrate or judge. In an affidavit for probable cause for the first search warrant at my work office and home, Detective Priest included what he said were Bernita's mother's dying words as, "Artis killed her." In order to obtain additional search warrants, a police officer should have fresh, new or additional information that is relevant to the case. Priest made the comment that I was not suspected of pulling the trigger, but I may have contracted with someone to kill Bernita. When investigators could not establish any proof I killed Bernita, they started searching for information to prove I hired someone. In an affidavit to search my vehicle, Priest changed Bernita's mother's last dying words from "Artis killed her" to "Artis had her killed."

This was the probable cause he swore to in front of a judge to obtain a search warrant to search my vehicle a second time. Changing the verbiage in this manner suggests there is information I contracted the murder. If that were true, the police could swear to another warrant and search again. Of course, the information is not true. Normally, when a person is dying of a heart attack he/she is more concerned with how he/she can obtain help immediately. I don't believe that when my mother-in-law was dying she used her thought process to help the police solve the crime. Especially when days before Bernita's death Mrs. Sims mailed me a letter sending all her love to me. What Mrs. Sims said (if anything) while she was dying of a heart attack cannot be proved or disproved. No matter what was said, the information should not be conveniently changed by the police to execute search warrants.

Priest broke another golden rule of investigation: never try to make the crime fit the person. I don't know where he received his training, but I was not trained to start with a suspect and attempt to find a crime. I was always trained to start with the crime and find a suspect. Priest will never be punished for that intentional search warrant content mistake, even though he cannot ignore he typed this lie then changed it to another lie to freshen information for a new search warrant.

To the innocent person, this turns on the light. It is an alert that a person will do the wrong thing for a conclusion of a pre-determined outcome. This is a very dangerous posture for a person of power. As long as an officer is trying to do the right thing (in the eyes of the public), he gets the wink from the general population and justice system.

Detectives Priest and Hemmingway were so involved with their concerns that the issues of justice and fairness became secondary. The more complex and overburdened an investigation becomes, the less truth comes out.

Take a moment to reflect upon the Abner Louima case. This incident occurred in New York City where four New

York police officers were charged with assaulting Louima by shoving a wooden stick into his mouth and rectum while he was handcuffed. The Abner Louima case is a prime example of police officer brutality. In my opinion, the officers who beat and punished Louima committed the crime not because they thought they were going to get away with it. Eventually, they knew they would get caught. If Louima lived, he would tell. They did it because they believed nothing was going to happen to them once they were found out.

This is a serious problem given the fact that police officers have so much power. It is also very similar to the Bernita's case, but on a lower scale. There is no difference between renegade New York police officers who beat a person for the shear enjoyment and an LPD officer padding information to obtain search warrants. The mentality is the same.

This mentality is guarded by the fact that the public (mostly) supports the police. We, as citizens, know that police officers have a difficult job. Therefore, we believe that if a police officer is doing his job, at times it is fair for that police officer to bend the rules as long as he is doing his best to catch the bad guy. Although a detective's professional ethics would seem to forbid such behavior, there is no clear line between acceptable detective hardball tactics and misbehavior.

I say that type of behavior is not acceptable. It is not permissible for police officers to cross the line, even momentarily, in support of doing their jobs. That has certainly happened in the Bernita White case. Too much responsibility has been given to untrained officers by prosecutors and judges to obtain investigative subpoenas and search warrants. There is a certain amount of leniency by judges and prosecutors for murder cases. That is to be expected. How a police officer uses this option is crucial.

I allowed investigators to enter my house to search my belongings and remove items they believed to be important for the investigation. They did not take that opportunity to search my house thoroughly. They only wanted my computer and van. I promptly signed the paperwork to allow them to remove these items.

When I arrived home on that fateful day, Mia "The Glue," Karen, my nieces, and my daughters were all in the house. After the officers left the house, all of us just sat down and stared. We tried our best to explain to Alanna and Michala. It was the most heart-wrenching conversation I have ever had to have. How do you tell your daughters that their mother and grandmother were taken away from them? I didn't have the answers. We didn't have the answers. A quick briefing in general was all that we could give. The rest would have to come in the morning.

I don't know why anyone attempted to go to sleep that night. No one slept. I woke up the next morning and read the newspaper. That morning was my first training session with the good and evil of the media. Reporters are an entirely different breed of people. I must give them credit for their persistence, stubbornness and the ever-present preservation of the right to know. I'm all for it. It is my motivation for writing this book. In less than two years, I have had the opportunity to critique reporters.

I must say that most of them have been very good. All of them want to get the story first. I question their dedication to getting the story correctly, but I understand their pressures. There is plenty of competition in their field. One station even secretly recorded my conversation and played the audio portion for the nightly news. While that is not illegal, it is certainly not ethical.

The important aspect to remember about news reporting is a reporter does not necessarily report stories as much as he gathers quotations from two or more people in disagreement. It is not his job to discover the truth. It is the reporter's duty to preserve our right to know. When the truth is not as amusing as our right to know, the news is only provided for entertainment.

As a person who has been interviewed by the media on several occasions, I have learned to hope they videotape my good side. Ultimately they will err, you can only hope it is in your favor. How does the expression go? "How long can the media keep you as front page top story news?" As long as they want to is the answer.

CHAPTER NINE

"Where every something, being blent together turns
to a wild of nothing."   —William Shakespeare

"We believe he knows who did it. He just won't tell us."

How would you like to be in the gumshoe's shoes right now? One year after Bernita's death, 9000 investigative hours, 500 people interviewed, 28 subpoenas and search warrants and you are no closer to solving this crime as the day you first started.

Let's attempt to think like the LPD detective in this self-imposed predicament. Walk in his shoes, think like him, and look through his eyes. You are he.

First, you can't retreat because nobody showed you how. Besides, it looks bad to say you wasted time and money on the wrong person while the real killer is living a normal life. You are at a tug of war with no rope; in the beginning you are amusing. After awhile, you just look stupid. You feel the pressure from upper command to solve the case because you have two other unsolved murders.

So, you made a few mistakes, huh? Changed a few words on a search warrant, illegally used a person's credit history, and hope to embarrass witnesses into telling the truth? Not a bad idea if it would have worked. After all, you are doing the best you can with what you have. The public would have excused your errors if you made an arrest by now. It's a tough job and somebody has to do it. If you can't win, don't lose, right? Maybe you can get promoted out of the detective division and do a good job, just like Detective South. You have more experience than he does, hands down.

You could have done a better job without the state police butting in. It's your case. They should go back to driving up and down on the expressway writing tickets. Who let D/Sgt. Hornberg speak on the local news to discuss your case like it was his? Why did the Chief hire that private detective? Does he not have any faith in you or does he think you need all the help you can get?

Oh well, wait a couple of months and the overtime budget will get approved, the PI will be gone and you will be back in the overtime saddle once again. Milk it for what you can. Overtime has never been so easy for a case this size.

Now, place yourself in my shoes. It is also a bad predicament, but it is not self-imposed. No one wished this to happen to me, but it has happened nonetheless. One year later and I am suddenly single, a widower, raising two young daughters all alone. I have lost my wife and my mother-in-law in an instant. My family is supportive. I have made it through a year, but many questions that have not been answered. Why did this have to happen? Why did this have to happen to me? Can I make it on a single-family income? Can I borrow any more money? What happens when the medical coverage for therapy for the girls and me runs dry? Will my kids ever understand? Will anyone ever know the answers to these questions?

No one should ever have to live long enough to experience what my family and I have been through during this investigation. It has been exhaustive and mentally draining for everyone. No one knows how to deal with the psychological and physiological stress one goes through when a wife/mother and mother-in-law/grandmother's life is snatched away too soon. Too soon, like a birthday cake full of candles that are snuffed out before you have the chance to wish for the future.

I never thought I would be raising two children by myself. Even though Bernita and I had decided to divorce, we always intended on raising the children together. We both had excellent parental skills. No one should be forced into raising children alone. It should be a choice. I never had that choice. It is difficult raising two daughters especially when you are a male. If I did not have the proper family skills I learned on the farm, I would never have made it. I pride myself on setting a good example for my kids. I enjoy cooking, so I'm teaching them to cook. I respect a well-maintained household, so I'm teaching my children how to clean. I believe it is important to ask for respect from others, so I do not use foul language, drink, or smoke.

No matter what template you use to raise your children, only half of your efforts will result in success. The other half is determined by what your children want to do. I have been blessed with two great children. As much as we have been through together, I have had the comfort of knowing my children will make it through this. We will move on to worry about other important categories such as if they should wear the color black with navy blue.

What was a struggle and continues to be is their hair. You may not think this is a big issue, but that's a lot of hair for a dad to handle! During the funeral arrangements, I was like a chicken without a head running 100 mph backwards.

Mia, "The Glue," told me not to worry about the hair. "You have way too many other things to think about now." She said.

"Mia. I can't do it. I've never combed their hair into any type of style. I mean, I can give them a battlefield ready hairdo, but I don't really know what I'm doing."

"There are enough women in this family to give you all the help you need," she said cracking a little smile.

The day of the funeral everything was rushed and hectic. The media was having their day. Photographers were everywhere. My youngest daughter Michala needed to used the restroom. She went on her way with Mia. Michala's hair, for lack of a better term, was running its own program. In other words, her hair was all over her head. Mia, "The Glue," looks at me and says, "Artie, you need to worry about her hair."

"It's on my to do list," I said confidently.

What is not easy to accept are the reactions of my friends and co-workers. Trauma has a way of bringing out the truth in people. People just do not know how to act. There are no instruction manuals. No one tutors you for the right thing to say. Shortly after the incident, I was placed on paid investigatory leave, not administrative leave.

Investigatory leave means the department places an employee on paid leave while they look into a suspicious activity. It protects the department while the suspicious activity is being investigated. Administrative leave is very similar but the employee is on paid leave for reasons other than suspicious activity.

I didn't request any leave but, notwithstanding, I was given the time off. MSP management arrived at my house to retrieve my service weapon and badge. I didn't have either.

My gun and badge were under lock and key at the office. For practically four months, I patiently waited for the case to come to fruition. Every night I went to sleep at 2:00 am wondering why it happened. I woke up at 5:00 am wondering who did it.

WHO KILLED MY WIFE?

The mini-vacation wasn't bad, but it was eating away at me not being on the front lines looking for the killer. As the progress of the case slowly ground to a crawl, I watched as the public shook their heads in a confused state. Friends started to categorize and separate. Some visited to be nosey. Some came by in hopes of being in the know. Others visited as if nothing ever happened. I have not seen some since June 23, 2001. These are the people struggling with their own emotions.

Just as the police are not trained to retreat, others are not trained to engage. They simply do not know what to say and I do not hold a grudge for that, especially when investigators are interviewing people and relaying they will arrest me in two weeks. Most of my friends are not police officers. They are not familiar with answering questions posed by the police. Most friends were more than willing to be interviewed and polygraph tested with hopes of steering the investigation in the right direction. What was disturbing was watching my friends who I thought were my good friends scatter like ants on an anthill.

In the back of their minds was the possibility I was guilty. An association with guilt in any form is not socially accepted nor will it help upwardly mobile, career motivated employees. I don't know which was more entertaining to watch; those who didn't know what to say, those who said what they didn't know, or those who hoped no one was looking when they said anything to me.

The most entertaining moment happened during a conversation with MSP F/Lt. Eddie Washington and me. I dropped in to see F/Lt. Washington who is the Commander of the MSP Detroit Post. I've known Eddie for years. He used to come by my house, ask me how the kids were, and send me E-mails, the usual things that friends do.

That day I showed up unannounced with Michigan State University Criminal Justice intern Tracey Bentz. Eddie gave me a big manly hug and said, "I've been praying for you."

"Where have you been? How come you don't call anymore"? I said.

"It's not like we were that close to begin with."

"I thought we were. I can't verify you were praying for me but it doesn't matter now."

I left with a wide-eyed intern in close proximity. I haven't talked to Eddie since.

Granted, most people do not know what to do or say with a case like this, but I have had the opportunity to realize who my close friends are. I spent almost four months on paid leave during the first part of the investigation. I was straining at the leash to get back to work. On the other hand, I was worried that if someone targeted Bernita, then it would follow that someone may target my children or me.

I was constantly on alert. Four months had passed since I spent six hours talking to the LPD investigators on the night the shooting occurred. Information was starting to come back to me that LPD planned to arrest me in two weeks. I don't know if that was some sort of scare tactic but to me it was an alert that investigators may be attempting to fabricate evidence to support a case. After all, where was the evidence? If we outline the facts, here is what we see.

- June 23, 2001, at Potter Park marked one of the most unusual, bizarre homicides that the state of Michigan has ever witnessed.

  Immediately following the shooting, people were running everywhere. Elena Paizana was walking in Potter Park when she heard a shot. Shortly after the shooting, fifteen Lansing police cars whizzed past her and told everyone to get out. Adam Gurski was there also and heard a park official over the intercom order everyone to leave.

  Potter Park's contractual security patrol locked the gates before anyone could leave. When LPD arrived, their officers opened the gates and waved everyone through. They forfeited a chance to interview hundreds of patrons as they treated the incident as a barricaded sniper.

- On June 28, 2001, investigators searched for the missing bullet in a river that flowed nearby. LPD joined forces with MSP detectives to form an eleven-man taskforce. The taskforce searched the area and found a tree with a small hole consistent with a possible bullet hole. After cutting the tree down and X-raying a section of the tree, investigators concluded the hole was a result of a drill bit, possibly from the Forestry Department. Attendance at Potter Park dropped between twenty and thirty percent even though LPD increased the bike and motorcycle patrols at the park.

- On July 6, 2001, a search warrant was served on me allowing officers to search my residence. It was quite a spectacular show conducted right in front of my children. Mia, "The Glue," happened to be downstairs when it happened.

"Artie, the police are here."

I yelled downstairs, "How many?"

"All of them," she said calmly.

"It's probably just the search warrant. Ask them if they want anything to eat."

Detectives didn't remove much of anything during the search. I was more than a little disturbed that LPD took my digital camcorder and every videotape I owned. Every birthday party and Christmas was kept in those memoirs. It wasn't much but it was everything I had. A few other odds and ends were also removed. The items have never been returned.

- On July 11, 2001 Raymond Townshend, a MSP retired crime scene investigator and forensic expert examined the scene. Townshend concluded that the shooter was a gun expert who knew what he was doing. Neither LPD nor MSP would comment on Townshend's announcement. Nobody knew what prompted his arrival. Nobody knows if he was paid to offer his opinion or what his rationale was.

- On July 12, 2001, Carol Webster, executive director for the Potter Park Zoological Society, admits that smaller crowds are visiting the zoo this year. However, Murdock Jemerson, Director of Lansing Parks and Recreation, declares that the parks are safe as ever.

- On July 19, 2001, a special dog was brought in by Sandy Anderson of Great Lakes Canine Services. The K-9 was trained to sniff out human tissue. If a bullet were left at the scene of the crime, the dog would be able to locate it. The dog found a metal piece that investigators claim may be the bullet used in the shooting. The K-9 found it within 15 minutes of the search but located the metal further north than anticipated.

- On August 2, 2001, Investigators announce I had a motive and say I had enough time to fire the shot, even though witnesses place me at the Delta Mills Park miles away, shortly after the shooting.

- On August 6, 2001, LPD had a search warrant to search the van I drove to the park on June 23, 2001. On June 23, 2001, I gave consent to search the vehicle. They kept the van for a month. Investigators say it is important to retrieve information from the vehicle's Alpine Navigational System to disprove where I said I drove the van after I left Potter Park.

- On August 8, 2001, Detective Priest announced that I might have contracted someone to kill Bernita. He further stated I am not suspected of pulling the trigger, but I may know who shot Bernita.

- On August 22, 2001, Lt. Hall commented about the metal fragment found at the zoo. "It's a bullet, but we are unable to conclude if it's a bullet used in this homicide. We're simply not sure why the dog hit on the fragment, it could be the residue from another source like an animal."

- October 9, 2001, I returned to work. LPD announces I remain on a "short list of suspects."

- On October 17, 2001, I turned over my department-issued handguns to D/Sgt. Sam Hornberg who test fired the guns, four months after the shooting.

- October 18, 2001, I offered a $5,000 reward for any information leading to the arrest of the perpetrator in this case. No calls were made to the Lansing police number given for the reward. In February of 2002, Detective Sergeant David Larnz, case officer in charge, called me and asked if I received any calls concerning the reward. According to Larnz, no one had called.

- October 31, 2001, Halloween. An investigative subpoena is issued which ordered my two children to answer questions about the day of the murder.

- August 28, 2002, 15 detectives for 13 months have spent

9000 hours investigating, interviewed 500 people, obtained and served 20 search warrants and 12 investigative subpoenas, and the zoo shooting remained unsolved. Chief Matt Alloy said, " Authorities invested more time and resources into White's death than for any city homicide in memory." Jay Siegal, Michigan State University professor of criminal justice and expert on physical evidence said, "This is a very cold crime scene at this point. It's the most frustrating kind of crime, and it may never get solved. That's the most likely scenario."

What went wrong?

CHAPTER TEN

"The public will believe anything as long as it is not
founded on truth."   — Edith Sitwell

For many people, the fear of the unknown is the greatest
fear. For me it is the opposite. I fear the known. I know that an
alarming percentage of murder cases are not solved. I know
that the longer it takes to solve the crime, the more difficult
the case becomes. I also know that when a police department
begins to speculate and draw conclusions based on
uneducated hunches, the "*Thin Blue Line*" has been crossed.

From the very beginning, this case was like a grocery
cart with a wobbly wheel. You keep pushing even though
it's not going in the right direction. If you let go, it will go in
any direction it wants. But, if you take the time to stop and
fix it, it will go in the right direction. It's time to fix the wheel.

The area where Potter Park is located is in a less than
favorable area. The security at Potter Park has mentioned
they have requested LPD to respond to several "shots fired"

complaints. Luke, a good friend of mine and a LPD officer told me shots ring out over there all the time.

Potter Park security told me that sometimes LPD responds, sometimes they don't. One of the security officers for Potter Park called me at work to explain what he found. He told me during his regular patrol of the park (and just after the shooting) he found a large piece of carpet on the ground. The grass underneath the carpet was still green and fresh. He located a dead squirrel in the path where investigators say the shot came from. He said the squirrel appeared to have been shot. He went to investigators with the information and they refused to interview him

Why did police rush everyone out of Potter Park without properly interviewing everyone? Nobody knows the answer to that one. Why did it take so long for investigators to interview witnesses who could immediately clear me? Shortly after the incident, several people showed up at my house. The common complaint was "What are they (LPD) doing?" "Who are they looking for?"

Bill Hay was walking with Bernita when she was shot. Bill called me and said, "The police are not looking in the right direction." He wanted to talk about it in person. Bill came over to my house to explain. He said he was pushing his son in a stroller and talking to his brother, John, who was walking between him and Bernita. While he was talking, Bill said he heard what sounded like a firecracker. The noise was loud, loud enough for him to look down on the ground next to him. He thought "You can't go anywhere without somebody doing something."

John heard the shot also, and he wears two hearing aids. The shot was either very loud, or relatively close. Bill said the three of them were walking in a line with his son slightly in front. The children, including Michala were ten feet in front of the group, playing with each other. When he heard the shot, he looked down to his left. He heard Bernita scream and saw her raise her hands in the air.

"John! Get the kids! They're shooting!" he said. John ran forward to get the kids and Bill held Bernita and allowed her to fall to the ground. A person who identified herself as a nurse ran over to help. Bill told everyone to leave because there could be more shots fired. In his haste to rush to Bernita's aid, Bill forgot about his son who was left alone in the stroller. He yelled for a stranger to take his child to safety. Bill said Bernita took one last breath and died quickly, in his arms.

I only listened when he told me what happened that day. I never interjected. Death is tragic, but it is the reality that one rash act, one thoughtless moment, can change so many lives. The short amount of time my family was allowed to grieve was overshadowed by suspicion and doubt. I often wondered if I were not a police officer would the investigative manpower hours be the same as the other unsolved murders in Lansing, Michigan.

The sole purpose of this book is to direct attention to the Bernita White case, afresh: to review the facts, rethink the present principles and to ask if the investigators are doing their best.

My struggle is in my commitment to search for the truth. Therefore, I am forced to sit and wait while unskilled investigators look truth dead in the eye and ignore its presence. That was the behavior throughout this investigation. The investigators made no distinction between hunches and real evidence. Everyday for almost two years, detectives tiptoed on the *thin blue line*, crossing over from time to time, only to confuse the judgment of the average citizen.

Truth is 100 percent, 100 percent of the time. It's not 70 percent or 99 percent, for that matter. The truth cannot be learned until LPD admits their mistake. They must come forward and announce they have no idea who committed this crime. It would be an honorable and noble gesture on their part. That statement would give me a sense of satisfaction that investigators are now willing to look for the truth. No one can find the killer until they (LPD) look for him.

LPD can continue to pretend they are "getting close", will "arrest me in two weeks" and keep me on the "short list of suspects", for the rest of forever because the statute of limitation for murder allows them to do that. The case can remain open and they can feign they are following a lead. I am counting on the rest of the world to be curious and ask the question… "Where is the evidence?" That would be a start in the right direction to find the truth, because you cannot find the truth unless you look for it. I want to say that the search for truth goes hand in hand with the search for justice.

I believe that political interest and unchecked police power can obscure the truth. A good investigator has a knack for acquiring information. Most successful investigators have the capacity for acquiring a 'feel' or 'street savvy.' We learn to ride a bike by riding a bike. We learn how to investigate by investigating. The greatest investigators are smart, acute listeners, detailed evidence gatherers, and superior at asking the right questions.

Which finally brings me to the comic relief of this book and to the complete opposite of the above description; Doug Mancino, CIFI, CFE, PI Director, Special Investigations, Prudential Financial.

One year into the investigation of my wife's death, I went to my chain of command at MSP for answers. I felt that six months was enough time to clear a suspect if not find the criminal. I talked with D/F/Lt. Ken Knowlton. Knowlton had always been a fair person when I worked with him on the road. He was close to retiring. He was also the command officer in charge of the MSP detectives assigned to the task force investigating the case. Nonetheless, I trust him. During that conversation he told me that LPD Chief Alloy was not satisfied with the results of the investigation by his detectives. Alloy hired a private investigator by the name of Doug Mancino. Mancino was described as a seasoned investigator with 28 years of homicide investigations.

Mancino was working for an insurance company after working as a detective for the Sterling Heights Police Department in Sterling Heights, Michigan. Knowlton directed me to give Sgt. Larnz at LPD a call, so I did. Larnz told me Mancino was available for me to speak with. I could tell Larnz didn't like it, having a private person come all the way from Minnesota to work on the case. After all, Sgt. Larnz was the last remaining investigator to say he was in charge. In the beginning, five people were announcing they were in charge. Now, only one admits it. I'll give Larnz credit for that.

I was impressed with the opportunity to speak with a homicide expert. I was informed Mancino was an independent investigator working independently from the task force. I was an impressed skeptic. After all, what more could one additional person working alone do? It was odd that Mancino was hired not as a consultant, but as an independent investigator. Most experts in the field work with local investigators to provide a different aspect of the investigation that others may have missed.

I didn't have anything to lose. My only stipulation was I refused to be treated like a suspect. LPD had mentioned to D/F/Lt. Knowlton that they had a few questions they wanted to ask that only I had the answers to. If it was to help the investigation, I was all for it. That was the only reason I agreed to meet with the private investigator.

After all, LPD did promise to arrest me in two weeks.

What kind of questions did they want to ask me after threats like that?

I was anxious to meet the veteran investigator. Since Mancino was also an insurance investigator, I brought my life insurance forms for him to review. A person "on a short list of suspects" is still a suspect. When a police department reports their unsupported, uneducated hunches to the life insurance companies "suspects" don't receive their life insurance claims as beneficiaries. Insurance companies are careful not to pay the wrong person for fear of having to pay again to the correct person.

I wanted to show my claims to the Prudential Financial Director of Special Investigations, Doug Mancino, CIFI, CFE, PI. I spent two days with the man who has more letters *behind* his name than I have *in* my name. When we first met, we immediately started assessing each other. He didn't look like a highly skilled investigator, but looks can be deceiving. He dressed cheaply like a typical police officer but sometimes we police officers don't like to get all dressed up.

The first time he opened his mouth to speak was his last opportunity to come off as a highly skilled sleuth. Prudential Financial Director of Special Investigations, Doug Mancino, CIFI, CFE, PI. was nothing more than a part time private investigator.

I realized I had wasted my time about the same time Chief Alloy realized he paid too much money for this gumshoe. I was embarrassed to be spending my time with him. He had no clue. He had no direction and he was lacking in skills. To this day I don't know why he was hired.

We went through the normal question and answer period. He couldn't help me with my life insurance questions, but he kept the information in the back of his head. I went with him to Potter Park Zoo. It was the first time I went to Potter Park since the shooting. We even drove in his car along the route I vaguely remembered driving from the park that day. Then, the comedy began. Mancino was faced with a few logistical problems. The area where he showed me he believed the killer took the shot from was not within eyeshot of both the zoo and the pavilion. Keeping with the high-powered rifle theory, a person would have to wait for the victim to walk to the zoo from the pavilion. If the killer didn't know the victim was coming to the zoo, he would have to take the shot at the pavilion because he can't shoot and hit a target at both locations from where Mancino said the perpetrator took the shot. (Alas! If a killer was to specifically target a person at the zoo, he would have to know when that person was due to arrive.)

Now, Mancino had to put me in the picture, show me the evidence and make me confess. His entire goal was to ask me why I didn't kill Bernita, and then poke holes in my story.

It just didn't work. I didn't have any reasons why I didn't or wouldn't kill my wife. When you are innocent, you don't have to make up stories. It's easy to stick with one story, the truth. "I didn't kill her because I didn't do it." I could tell he was getting frustrated with me. We were getting nowhere so I thought I would play his game as long as I didn't miss my lunch and the weather became too cold.

He wanted to know why I didn't show more concern for Michala on the day Bernita died. I knew Michala was in good hands because Harris told me his wife Kim was with her. I trust Harris with my life. I trust Kim with all my heart. That wasn't an issue. Mancino didn't like that answer.

He also placed a lot of importance on June 22, 2001, the day before Bernita's death. I remember the day only as a race day. I drag race a street car. That's my hobby. I never raised a wrench on a vehicle before I started working on my 1987 Buick Grand National. I soon joined a Buick Grand National Club and was elected president of the club where I am the president in good standing.

A few of our members met at the Milan Dragway on that Friday to tune our cars. It was an average day for me — it was a workday, the kids went to school. Sometimes, the kids and Bernita joined me at club functions. Since this meeting in Milan was not a Club-sponsored event, I went alone that night.

The car didn't run well that evening. I was trying to push the car to its limits and as a result, I hurt the engine and blew a head gasket. Club member Mike Lambert gave me a hand with the car so I could limp it home, adding water to the coolant system the entire way. I was happy to get the car home without hurting it further.

WHO KILLED MY WIFE?

Mancino believes—and accused me of—driving to Potter Park Zoo on this evening to position a rifle with a scope so that I could execute the crime the next day. This is simply not true.

He seemed concerned with my inability to supply more details. He made a comment that if it happened to him, he would remember everything that happened the day before, during, and after. I remember going to the drag strip and racing my car and barely making it back home due to engine problems. I never had to retrace my steps because it's not important. I don't have anything to cover for. I don't need to create a story and stick with it to cover anything. A guilty person needs to create a story or alibi, memorize it and never deviate from it.

The funniest comment Mancino made was I was so intelligent, I could mastermind the entire caper and get away with it. Me? So intelligent? I told him "Thanks for the complement, but my entire family would beg to differ with you. They don't think I'm smart at all!"

Next, Mancino was ready to move in for the kill. It was confession time. He actually wanted me to confess to the crime. I laughed in his face when he told me how it was done.

Here's Prudential Financial Director of Special Investigations, Doug Mancino, CIFI, CFE, PI's rendition of what happened.

He starts off, "Before today, there was only one person who knew who did it. Now there's two."

Where did he get that rehearsed prom date pickup line from, I thought to myself. He went on to say how I did it. He reiterated his theory that on Friday June 22, 2001, I drove to Potter Park Zoo and hid a high-powered rifle with a scope in the woods. Then on June 23, 2001, just before my departure, I told Michala my five-year-old that she really, really wanted to go to the zoo, so she would start crying and make Bernita take her. Then I drove to the Park, used the rifle, and took the shot. He ended his monologue with. "I just don't know what you did with the gun."

I burst into laughter inside and out. After I stopped laughing, I told him "You know, ten months ago if you would have told me that, we would be rolling around on the grass right now." I gave him a long pause to see if I scared him.

I continued " But you are just another person with another opinion. There isn't enough evidence to arrest the person who did it, let alone me."

From there, he just continued trying to get me to confess to his whimsical story. All along, I'm thinking what kind of fool would believe I could prompt a five-year-old to cry on key and make all of this happen? I continued to think to myself... I wonder if the Chief paid him all this money because they are related?

Mancino really started to get desperate, "I see your lip trembling. Is this where we roll on the grass?"

I replied, "No, I'm cold. You won't know when we'll roll on the grass. I'll just sucker punch you."

He began begging me for a confession. He looked like one of those circus seals balancing a ball on his nose, waiting for approval and a piece of fish. There really wasn't a difference except a seal would wear better clothes.

I was disappointed. I was led to believe I would be talking to an expert who could help solve the crime. Instead, I wasted two days to be accused of murder. D/F/Lt. Knowlton said Chief Alloy spent thousands of dollars on Prudential Financial Director of Special Investigations, Doug Mancino, CIFI, CFE, PI. The truth about Mancino is he was never a homicide investigation expert.

In fact, he only spent a few years with the Sterling Heights Police Department before he went to Prudential Financial. I never saw him again and nobody mentions his name.

CHAPTER ELEVEN

"I hear and I forget. I see and I believe. I do and I understand."   — Confucius

A year and a half after Bernita's death and there are no answers. The murder task force that once had as many as fifteen people has dwindled to just a few who meet every two weeks. Most officers on the case have either accepted a promotion, retirement, or transfer. I am left with nothing but humiliation and disgruntlement as I float atop this sea of suspicion. There are no new developments and no explanations as to why everything went wrong.

The fact remains, there is no bullet, no gun, no eyewitness, no DNA evidence, no motive, and no suspect; at least not a feasible one. The attendance rate at Potter Park Zoo is back to normal. I'm positive Management at the zoo would like to forget this ever happened. I can't. What did happen?

It is a fact that Bernita was shot in the arm. The bullet went through her arm, pierced her heart and exited the right side of her body. Investigators believe a high-powered rifle was used at a long distance. Why did eyewitnesses at the scene believe the shot was much closer? Without the bullet or gun, it is difficult to draw conclusions. Many authorities believe that a trained sniper would never risk shooting a person in the arm. The bullet could be deflected off the large bone in the arm.

Where is the proof that would support the sniper theory? The dog used to sniff out human tissue did find a bullet. The DNA from the flesh on the bullet did not match Bernita's DNA. How many more human flesh covered bullets could be found at Potter Park Zoo if they took the time to look? Where is any evidence that Prudential Financial Director of Special Investigations, Doug Mancino, CIFI, CFE, PI may have discovered?

Investigators say I know my wife's killer. What makes it convenient for them to say I did it, I had someone do it, and I know who did it? There is no proof to support either statement, but the comments keep me conveniently suspicious in the public view. Attempting to force the crime to fit the person never works. That investigative technique is as reliable as the criminally shaped skull theory, where some scientist believed the shape of a person's skull determines if they have criminal intentions.

What is the secret that LPD is keeping from the public? Why do they maintain they have important information imperative to the case but can't allow anyone to know? An even more curious question is where is LPD Management? Where are the Lieutenants? Where is a Captain? Where indeed is the Chief? The high-ranking officers, who must read the reports, must themselves be feeling the pressure of these questions. These questions cannot be resolved by simply releasing a statement to the press.

It is quite apparent that LPD has no evidence whatsoever.

If they had any evidence against me, I would have been arrested a long time ago. The big question is why do they continue to try to make my life miserable. They search my van and search it again, keeping it for six months. They force me to pay a $107 towing fee to pick up my vehicle they towed. They removed the van's navigational device in an attempt to disprove where I indicated I drove after leaving the park. That effort proved nothing. The navigational device also controls my climate adjustments. It was too cold to drive the van during the time the system was away.

They conduct a search in front of my children and remove my expensive video camera and all of my home videos of the kids. They even took Michala's crayon drawing and my wedding band. Since, apparently they are not required to leave an inventory of what they take while executing a search warrant, I don't know if the ring was stolen or not. Just as the Grinch stole Christmas, you can't keep Christmas from happening. I used a disposable camera to capture the memories of my daughters coming down the stairs on Christmas morning December 25, 2001, just as I have done for years.

The Dial Number Recorder (DNR) a device that records my outgoing and incoming phone numbers to the police is still on my phone. America On Line (AOL) allowed investigators to seize my account. Police continue to monitor my E-mail messages on my new account. I haven't changed my mannerisms on the phone or E-mail.

I don't have to watch what I say or do. Sometimes I E-mail the people I don't care for to ensure they will get an interview by the police. They did return my computer. I still can't get it to work. All of these minor inconveniences wouldn't bother a guilty person. The guilty person would have other things to worry about. For the innocent person, it is a big deal. It is one thing to assist with the investigation but another to have to buy new running shoes, camera, computer, etc. because the police have the option to keep your property.

From the woman behind the meat counter at Meijer's, to the retired MSP Lieutenant, I still hear comments. The woman behind the counter who sold Bernita and I meat and fish for years asked where Bernita was one day. I told her she was killed at Potter Park. She looked at me in a confused state and said, "But they said the husband did it."

Then there was Randy Fayling (MSP retired Lieutenant). I was working in Flint, Michigan when I stopped to talk to Randy. I have known Randy for years. His wife Leslie was my secretary for four years. We talked for about ten minutes before he says, "Just like that guy in Lansing who smoked his wife. Everybody knows he did it. They just can't prove it."

"Randy, that's me they are talking about," I said.

"I guess I really put my foot in my mouth, huh?"

"No, you are no different than anyone else with an opinion. You just came out and said yours."

When people believe you are being investigated for murder, it can give you a sense of power. For so many years, I was the good guy chasing down the villains. Now, at least a few people think I am a bad guy.

At times when I walk into a room and a silence comes over the crowd, I feel arrogant. Other times I feel fear knowing that lethal mistakes have been made by the police that may never be corrected. Mostly, it is a feeling of relief that if any comfort was to ever surface from this it is the pride I get from my daughters' ability to adjust. When everything is said and done, that's all that matters. They are the real troopers.

An Investigative Subpoena is an order requested by a prosecutor to compel a witness to testify. You have to talk and you have to tell the truth. The prosecutor subjected both my daughters to this.

It was a very sad day to see my daughters forced to relive the day their mother was murdered so a MSP "Expert" could interrogate them. As a matter of fact, Investigative Subpoenas were used throughout this case in the form of a witch-hunt, revealing what was to be expected. Nothing. I was never offered an Investigative Subpoena that would order me to tell the truth with perjury being the punishment for lying. Could it be that no one wanted to hear the truth? Some witnesses were served with Investigative Subpoenas, submitted to polygraph examinations, and interviewed up to five times. I suggest that was little bit of overkill for the results to be nil.

I never prompted any witnesses. Everyone I know was eager to be interviewed by the task force to tell the police I was not involved. Most witnesses and friends of mine are not police officers but pleaded to share their theories with the police until they were treated badly. Almost every person I know who was interviewed complained of being bullied, embarrassed, or threatened. After being treated badly, some refused to speak to the police again. Karen, a friend of mine testified for an Investigative Subpoena, and was interviewed three additional times. She refused to be interviewed again. Investigators threatened her with another Investigative Subpoena. She told them to "bring it on." She never heard from them again.

My friend, Marcia, was on a cruise ship when the shooting occurred. She received a polygraph, Investigative Subpoena and a couple of interviews. My good friend, Doc, received a polygraph, a couple of interviews and a strategically timed "sex question" in front of his wife that ruined his marriage. Misty was asked the "sex question,"

Lisa was asked the "sex question," Rebecca was asked the "sex question," Brenda was asked the "sex question," Marvel was asked the "sex question", and Rochelle was asked the "sex question". To sum the totals, all but a few of the women I know were asked if they had sex with me.

A pattern was soon developed by the murder task force. 1) Delay or avoid any witness who could prove my innocence. 2) Bully or embarrass every interviewee. Ask the sex question. 3) Use Investigative Subpoenas and polygraph examinations as threats to force people to talk. All of that was not necessary. Most people could not wait to talk but were surprised when no one listened. I cannot count the number of people who called me to comment on the lack of people skills the investigators had.

The scheduled interviews were illogical and haphazard. My sister, Karen, was never interviewed although her friend Mark was. I think I met him once. My sister, Angela, was never interviewed even though she dared New Jersey State Police to come to her door.

My brother, Mark, called with the news he was interviewed. "Did you run from the New Jersey detectives?" I asked jokingly.

"No, but your nephew was ready. Those were some big dudes."

"Did they ask you if we had sex?"

"Sick. They did ask me if I killed her."

"They ask everyone that one. Don't feel special. A few people have called to say LPD mentioned you didn't like her, for some reason."

"Why would they say that? I hardly talked to her. They didn't talk to mother."

"Why not?"

"They walked right past her, and asked to talk to me. I think they thought she was the neighbor lady because she looks so White."

"See? I told her to comb more coffee through her hair."

Mia, "The Glue." Piggee' called after her interview crying her eyes out. "Artie, they asked it."

"Let me guess. It was the sex question. Don't worry about it. You knew they would. Who was it?"

"Hemmingway and Handle. Handle ran out of here crying, telling me she was so sorry."

"Crying? What for?"

"She was just going on and on about how sorry she was. Hemmingway said he was going to arrest you in four weeks, and then he changed it to three weeks. He's an idiot."

"I think this is his first murder investigation. I asked some of the guys at the gym if he was a good investigator. They just told me he was a good golfer."

"You know with all these questions about sex, no

wonder they can't find the guy. They're just looking for a vagina. One big vagina running around with a disguise on."

"Beard, moustache, or both?"

A few of the investigators flew to Washington State to interview a friend whom I only have E-mail contact with. Ken, who works for Boeing Airlines, sent me an E-mail message to explain how the members of the task force and the Seattle police came to his home and workplace to interview him and his family. I felt sorry for him. For years he corresponded with me over the Internet with the sole purpose of helping me build a faster race car. He practically built my car over the Internet. Now, Ken had to endure having his son questioned about long guns while he had to take the time off work for a four-hour polygraph examination. Of course, he didn't mind because he wanted to help but you can imagine his job was a little curious. If you don't believe Big Brother is watching, send him E-mail.

My good friend, Phil Ferro, from Las Vegas called to tell me about his interview. Phil has about twenty-five years of real investigative experience. He is a highly skilled interviewer but was amazed at the briskness of both the LPD Officer and the MSP Officer who traveled to interview him. He said it was as if they had their gambling chips in their pockets, ready for the strip. He also complained how investigators showed up at his job creating a disturbance. After a few questions and a polygraph examination, they were on their way. He explained on the phone.

"I haven't seen you in years and they come way out here to talk to me."

"They sent two people all the way to Las Vegas to interview one person but can't send one person to New Jersey to interview six? I guess they really were not interested in what my family had to say."

"It's been a while since I had a bunch of badges pointed at me. I know you had nothing to do with anything but I live out here in Vegas. I was ready to confess to thirteen unrelated crimes."

"I bet you did. Did you pass?"

"Hell, yeah, I passed. They told me they knew everywhere I went because of my credit cards. I asked them why they were here if they knew everything? That's when they told me you were going to be indicted."

Some people who were interviewed never called. Most were intimidated when investigators told them not to contact me. It is part of the isolation the task force was attempting to create. Make the suspect feel like he's alone with no one on his side. Sometimes this tactic works against a guilty person who feels compelled to confess to the truth. For me, again, it's just annoying.

Only two people actually came forward and asked if I killed Bernita. Phil, who has a natural ability to read people, had to ask. He has been involved in the detective field longer than anyone knows. (Nobody really knows how old he is.) It was only natural that he would ask. He would not be able to live without knowing whether he was duped all these years by knowing me.

Harris was the other person who asked. Harris is a great friend but he is also a MSP command officer for the Polygraph Unit. He couldn't help it. "Why don't you take a polygraph? I can't do it because we are friends, but I can offer someone who can."

"Do you really think it matters if I take one and pass or fail at this point? They have already made up their minds. It won't matter one way or the other. Besides, Priest is lying on official documents. He's also stretching the timeline of the murder. Do you really think I should take one from a Department that allows that to happen or from a Department I'm suing?"

Harris received an interview. They never asked him to take a polygraph.

CHAPTER TWELVE

"The dead cannot cry out for justice. It is the duty of
the living to do so for them."
— Louis McMaster Bujold

Our justice system is not perfect. We live with
imperfections and injustices on a daily basis. Even when we
as police officers do our best, neither we, nor our behaviors
are perfect. Tolerating these imperfections does not in any
way suggest that I should abandon the pursuit of justice.
The truth will always be there and it cannot be ignored. Yet,
abandonment may seem to be the easiest way to cope with
this situation. If I do nothing, nothing happens. If I allow the
public to understand the ramifications of this case and the
impact it may have, the investigation may proceed in the
right direction.

Shortly after the murder, I sent out several surveys to
find out how the public felt about this case. I created a mailing
list of people to survey from the list of people who attended
Bernita's funeral. My strategy was to receive as many honest

and candid replies as possible. Since the list is the same list the task force used to begin their interviews, (LPD photocopied the sign-in sheet at the funeral home.) I felt it was appropriate. I was surprised at the openness of the returns. Most of the people surveyed did not respond.

Three percent of those who did respond received some type of police interview. (Some of my close friends were not surveyed because they verbally supplied their feelings.) In addition to a series of multiple-choice questions, the respondents were asked to share their personal theory as to who they believe is the perpetrator.

The Civil Litigation Theory was suggested. At least one of the responders felt that if a person was responsible for racial discrimination they might take drastic measures to protect their interests. Fearing a high dollar reward as a result of my winning the lawsuit could have forced that suspect to react. I cannot comment because the civil case is pending, however, I do not have any information to support that theory.

Several respondents suggested the Random Theory. Security at Potter Park reported several shots fired throughout the years at that location. LPD did find a bullet in the park revealing that the park employees are not strangers to violence. Because Potter Park Zoo has had several nearby complaints of gunshots, the Random Theory could be possible. Sandra Wagner writes:

> *"I feel my theory is one that the Lansing PD does not want to validate because of what the public reaction*

would be. I think that it was a random shooting, probably by some kid who will never confess. The question that came to mind, when they found the slug in the tree in the park, was how many other people have been shooting guns in the park? I feel the detectives came up with a theory right from the beginning. As they proceeded with the investigation, they were never able to look beyond that original theory."

The Boyfriend Theory was suggested by some of the respondents. Because of the lack of confidence in LPD's interview and interrogation skills there remains the possibility Bernita's male companion was not properly investigated due to the fact so much attention was given to me. Denise Shannon writes:

"I think that Bernita knew information that could have been incriminating information to someone involved in her workplace, either through her actual work or situations that might of happened outside of her work place. Bernita could have had dinner with a male co-worker, and that co-worker's wife found out and became jealous. This person must have been rich, because whoever shot Bernita was a skilled marksman. It had to be someone who knew Bernita's schedule. The marksman shot Bernita during daylight hours, and in a busy park."

Another theory suggests that the whole incident could have been a mistake. It is possible that a young child may have borrowed a family member's long gun for fun and made a mistake by firing the weapon. He may not even know he shot someone. This is very similar to the thought of a person high on drugs or a gang member taking a shot at anyone at the zoo. The person may not remember or even care he shot someone. Alexis Keep-Sparks writes:

"I think it has been so long and the police focused in one area too long. They clearly don't have any clues on where to go. Hiring a private investigator shows me they can't handle it and there were probably a lot of mistakes and issues that needed to be better investigated."

A few of the respondents suggested a surprising theory that deals with suicide. Because of Bernita's depression and the pending divorce, she may have arranged for the death herself. As with any of these aforementioned theories, this theory is only speculation. As I believe no one who knew Bernita would want to kill her, I also believe she would not want to take her own life because she loved her children immensely.

The volumes of people I have talked to all have their own beliefs. Not everyone agrees who the killer is. Whether the killer is an honest person who made an honest mistake, or a cold-blooded killer waiting for another opportunity to kill again, he still remains unknown.

Everyone agrees that the person who killed Bernita should not be able to walk our streets unaware of this travesty or feel he got away with murder.

WHO KILLED MY WIFE?

The fact remains that the killer walked away from Potter Park on June 23, 2001. It is essential to understand and realize we cannot progress until the remaining investigators on this case start over. We can go nowhere until they give up the façade of my continuation on the "short list of suspects." They can continue to pretend if we allow them.

There is no pressure for investigators to solve this case. There are no marches in front of the police precincts, no Civil Liberty Union interest, no family member pressures, no reason for them to look for the truth until now. I will never stop believing in the truth. Now is the time for everyone else who believes in the truth, to let it be known.

We can start with the first question. "Who Killed My Wife?" That question demands a response from LPD to answer the next questions: where is the evidence and where is the proof? Pretending to secretly have information imperative to the case is insufficient and professionally unacceptable. My family continues to live under the shadow of this tragedy. Eventually we will overcome this cloud and live normal lives again.

I continue to work as a police officer for a department that apparently does not believe I am a suspect for the simple reason I am still employed in the same capacity as before the sorrowful event. Nothing can be done until they stop investigating me. We know this is difficult. There are a number of mistakes that have to be admitted and that is not easily done. Historically, a police department never publicly admits its mistakes, but it is relative and important for this case.

Starting over is never wrong when the outcome can make everything right. Sometimes, you have to have the opportunity to get it wrong before you have a chance to make it right. I would not hold any detective accountable for taking charge and searching for the truth. However, not accepting responsibility for one's actions, right or wrong, is not a satisfactory response.

This book was designed in its entirety to educate everyone affected by this case and those who are unknowledgeable of police investigations. This is not only my objective, but that of thousands of people who want the truth to be discovered. From every unsolved murder right here in Lansing, Michigan to every person who has been slighted by unprofessional conduct by any public servant globally, we deserve the right to know the answer to: "Who Killed My Wife?"

The answer will be found when people ask the questions. Then the police must look for the answers.

I have developed a web site for anyone to go to if they have comments or clues. There, you can find frequently asked questions (FAQ) questions and answers, discussion groups and links to other similar web sites. It is http://www.artisticexpressions.org.

Additional information can also be forwarded to:

Artistic Expressions LLC
5115 Deanna Dr.
Lansing, MI 48917
Phone: 800 231-7959
Fax: 517 323-8375

I will personally return all correspondence.

At this time, I cannot offer a reward for any information leading to the arrest of the person responsible Bernita's death. Without life insurance I am suddenly raising two children on a single-family income. I have been forced to spend thousands of dollars on pending and new bills. My children and I are alone. Nevertheless, all of the proceeds (if any) from this book will go to solving this case.

If I did not have faith that this case would be solved, there would be no hope left for my family. Bernita is the victim but she does not suffer.

She is in heaven and she has no worries. The ones she leaves behind must endure the suffering. The percentage of unsolved murders is unacceptable. The Chandra Levy case and the Jon Benet Ramsey case both remain unsolved. There is still no resolution to Bernita White's murder. Unfortunately, murders will continue. Our perception of police will change with the times. Some crimes will go unsolved. I have faith that someday, someone will come forward and share what they know. Someone will shed light on the puzzle. The labyrinth of questions will never end until someone answers the question, "Who Killed My Wife?"

http://www.artisticexpressions.org

The truth... find it!

WHO KILLED MY WIFE?

ARTIS L. WHITE

Index

R
Reporters 74
reporters 75
reward 86, 112, 117

S
search warrant
    66, 67, 69, 71, 72, 73, 74,
    76, 77, 84, 85, 87, 102
security officers 89
Sergeant 2, 26, 69, 86
sex 64, 65, 105, 106, 107
sniper 83, 101
snitches 67
soap opera 63, 64
South Precinct 61
speculation 65, 114
Stereotyping 29
stereotyping 29
Sterling Heights Police
    Department 93, 99
strategy 65, 111
Subpoena 104, 105, 106
subpoena
    68, 69, 70, 74, 76, 86, 87
suspect
    26, 31, 35, 36, 37, 38, 41, 55,
    65, 66, 67, 71, 72, 86, 91,
    92, 93, 94, 100, 109, 112, 115
suspicious activity 80

T
taskforce 83, 112
tether program 9
Theory 112, 113
theory
    68, 95, 98, 101, 112, 113, 114
Thin Blue Line 88
thin blue line 22, 91
Tri-County Metro Narcotics
    36, 38
truth
    65, 66, 67, 69, 72, 75, 77, 80,
    88, 91, 92, 96, 99, 104, 105,
    109, 111, 115, 116, 118

V
victim 41, 54, 95, 117
videotape 75, 84
violence 112
volunteers 60

W
widower 77
wrongdoings 40

ARTIS L. WHITE

QUICK Order Form

WHO KILLED MY WIFE?
The Unsolved Murder of Bernita White $12.95

Email Orders: artisticexpressions.org
Fax Orders: 517-323-8375
Telephone Orders: 1-800-231-7959 (Have your credit card ready)
Postal Orders: Artistic Expressions LLC
        5115 Deanna Dr., Lansing, MI 48917

Please send FREE information on:
☐ Speaking/Seminars   ☐ Consulting   ☐ Guest Appearances

PLEASE PRINT CLEARLY

Name _____

Address _____

City/State/ZIP _____

Telephone (include area code) _____

Email address _____

HERE'S MY ORDER
"Who Killed My Wife? *The Unsolved Murder of Bernita White*"

_____ copies x $12.95 = $_____
Add 6% Sales Tax* $_____
Add Shipping* $_____
TOTAL AMOUNT: $_____

METHOD OF PAYMENT
☐ Check   Credit Card: ☐ VISA ☐ MasterCard ☐ AMEX

Card Number _____
Expiration Date _____
Name on Card _____
Authorized Signature _____

*Sales Tax: Please add 6% for products shipped to Michigan addresses.
**Shipping by Air: U.S. $4 for first book and $2 for each additional product.